That Reminds Me of the One...

That Reminds Me of the One...

True hunting & fishing
tales, misadventures,
and stupid stunts

WILLOW CREEK PRESS
Minocqua, Wisconsin

"The Heebie-Jeebies" by Jerry Dennis, excerpted from *A Place on the Water: An Angler's Reflections on Home*, by Jerry Dennis. Copyright 1993, St. Martin's Press.

ISBN 1-57223-024-X

Published by WILLOW CREEK PRESS
P.O. Box 147, Minocqua, WI 54548

For information on other Willow Creek titles,
write or call 1-800-850-WILD.

Library of Congress Cataloging-in-Publication Data

That reminds me of the one . . . : true hunting & fishing tales, misadventures, and stupid stunts.
     p.   cm.
   ISBN 1-57223-024-X (alk. paper)
    1. Hunting--Anecdotes. 2. Fishing--Anecdotes.
SK33.T44 1995
818'.5402--dc20   95-34047
                                   CIP

Printed in the United States.

Dedication

To Jim Bashline, in memorium.

Contents

vii

Foreword

Oh, for a life in the great outdoors. And what better occupation than that of an outdoor writer – fishing and hunting for a living, adventuring in exotic locales, experiencing a multitude of what would be, for the average sportsman, once-in-a-lifetime chances at trophy game and fish. Dream trips.

As some, maybe most, of the authors of this book will attest, the life of an outdoor writer is in fact enjoyable if not monetarily rewarding. But their lives are not without foibles, trials, and pains. Outdoor scribes are as susceptible as the average man to frustration, insect bites, fear, disorientation, searing heat, biting cold, bad luck, clumsiness, humiliation, anger, stupidity, remorse, and bewilderment. Yes, despite the admiration and honor heaped upon them, outdoor writers are mere mortals.

But you usually won't read about their foibles, trials, and pains in the magazines in which these writers' bylines appear. You will, however, in this book, where some of America's best hunting and fishing authors "fess up" to real-life hackle-raising moments, and even some rib-tickling incidents.

So be prepared in the following pages to be charged by bears, snakes, and African jackrabbits; to find yourself stranded in the desert and on the tundra, lost in the woods and on the water and in the air; to . . . well, we don't want to give it all away, do we?

–The editors

Terror In the Plowed Fields

Jim Bashline

For three weeks our small group of writer-explorers had enjoyed about as many moments of high adventure in Africa as most normal people could tolerate. Nick Sisley had been attacked on the Zaire River by freelance bandits, Bob Stearns was nearly lost at sea while battling a tarpon from a dug-out canoe at the mouth of Angola's Cuanza River, and Roger Latham experienced the thrill of having holes eaten into both legs by some unidentified swamp creatures in the rice paddies of Mozambique. Hair-raising (and hair-graying) events involving leopards, African ticks, unsociable baboons, Communist-led revolutionaries, and slowly-sinking boats in the Indian Ocean had become commonplace on this fact-finding trip. The running joke among our star-crossed group became, "Have you included me in your new will?"

Mark Sosin, Wally Taber, and I made up the rest of this African Lewis and Clark expedition that was enlisted to check out the bird-shooting and fishing possibilities in the, then, Portuguese protectorates of Angola and Mozambique. The trip had been organized by the Portuguese government and Fish and Game Frontiers, a fledgling travel group specializing in hunting and fishing treks. The month of March 1973 was selected as being a good weather period, and we were on our way.

The largest tarpon in the world were supposed to enter the Cuanza River for spawning duties, the largest bonefish in the world were supposed to swim in the bays of Mozambique, and both countries were supposed to hold an amazing combination of game birds and waterfowl. Some of these "supposed to's" proved to be true and some didn't. Ah, but as the tale-weavers like to say, "Those are other stories." This one is about a plowed field, or *shamba*, as they are called by the Bantus of Mozambique.

Considering the previous mishaps which befell our group, it seemed that the middle of a freshly plowed field would be a rather safe place to be. I was searching for such places during the last week of our stay mostly because my chances of getting out of Africa in one piece seemed to be shrinking.

Bird shooting over our professional hunter's English pointers began well. Franklin partridges were abundant on the edges of the shambas, where thick brush provided excellent cover. It wasn't unlike hunting the small farm fields of New England. The growth around the freshly turned shambas proved to be especially productive because of exposed worms and insects. The Franklins apparently enjoyed a touch of protein with their weed seeds and native corn.

The drill consisted of moving from one field to another, more or less following the dogs, while trying to remain in the open for easier shooting. Being in the plowed dirt most of the time was not done just for the shooting or more comfortable walking. It was also much easier to keep an eye out for annoying creatures that have a way of appearing at the damnedest times in Africa.

Wally and I were teamed this morning and, since we both had some experience with hunting dogs, were assigned a rack-ribbed white dog named Albert. Albert had dashed across the shamba at hand - every acre of this piece of real estate had a dozen 75-foot squares of cleared land - and skidded to a picture perfect point. I could see the dog's eyes rolling from side to side, an indication that there was a sizeable covey squatting in the monkeypod weeds. I brought the shotgun to high port position and stepped out smartly along the furrow I was in, both eyes glued to the dog's nose. Wally was about 25 feet behind me, slightly to my left, and on the move as well.

Two or three birds vaulted above the head-high

bushes,and I brought the gun to my shoulder. *BAM.*
But the sound didn't come from my gun! Chunks of
dirt and assorted flotsam struck the backs of both my
legs. My God, I've been shot!

I slumped to both knees, instantly sure that I had
just become a cripple for life. Wally must have fired at
the birds prematurely, and − oh shit! − I'm a hunting
accident victim in the middle of Mozambique. My
second reaction was to go for Wally's throat and stran-
gle him − if I could get on my feet and still walk.

A quick check of both legs revealed that I was not
bleeding. The dirt displaced by one and an eighth
ounces of No. 6 shot was what I'd felt. Four quick steps
toward Wally found me astraddle a well-ventilated
green mamba that later stretched out at about seven
feet. Wally was flat on his belly with his face buried in
the soft earth.

After we both regained some control over hearts
and nervous systems, Wally went over the sudden sce-
nario. When I began to trot towards the dog, I kicked
the mamba, which had been snoozing in the cool dirt.
I wasn't looking down. Mamba decided it didn't like
being trampled and took off after me. Wally didn't
think it was smart to holler because he was afraid I
might wheel and shoot towards him or there might not
be time to shoot before the snake nailed me. Good and
very quick thinking.

"I knew my angle wasn't perfect to hit the snake and avoid spraying you with some ricocheting pellets, but it was the only chance I had. I also thought it was a good idea to 'hit the dirt' the second I shot . . . just in case."

Remembering my first thoughts upon hearing the shot, this was still more good and quick thinking on Wally's part.

Considering the alternative, I'm extremely happy that Wally did what he did. According to most authorities, about four minutes is the allotted time for writing one's memoirs after a mamba says hello. In the will-writing game that evening I left my shotgun and soiled shorts to Wally.

(Even the last legs of this 1973 odyssey held surprises. Our flight from Angola to Lisbon had to turn around over the Atlantic and return to Luanda. There was a bomb on board!)

Troubled Waters

Chris Dorsey

After a hundred-mile float down Alberta's Wabasca River, we had the quartered carcasses and racks of a pair of bull moose stowed in our two 27-foot river canoes. Skinning, quartering, and packing a moose is typically a day-long affair, and we ran out of daylight as outfitter Weldon Prosser, his son Peter, and I finished distributing the ungulate cargo evenly between the two canoes.

A cold wind blew up before we could finish the chore and, with the canoes secured for the night, our next task was to build a fire while we could still feel our fingers. We warmed our hands over the flames, returning some semblance of manual dexterity to them—enough to tie down a pair of tents to house our slumber for the night.

Already a day behind schedule in reaching our pick-up point, but feeling rather adventurous, we reasoned that Lewis and Clark didn't hold to appointments either, and that a day or two extra in a voyage of this length wasn't anything unusual. Tired from the efforts of the day, however, we devoured supper before cocooning ourselves in goose down sleeping bags.

I awoke to the shouts of Weldon, whose earnest tone of voice suggested a forest fire or grizzly was approaching. Weldon is a skilled woodsman, and I didn't doubt that he had a perfectly reasonable explanation for wanting to get back on the river – pronto. I just didn't know what that reason was until I turtled my head out of the tent and saw the river. Only the night before, it was a peaceful, meandering stretch of water, but now large slabs of ice floated past our encampment, a foreboding suggestion of imminent freeze-up. Weldon had seen the river—the giver and taker of life that it is—like this before and knew we had to leave now or wait for rescue. There was no careful packing of the tents and no washing the skillet. They were thrown in a heap and jammed into a hole between two hind quarters in the closest canoe.

Once underway, we floated with the ice down the river. The sound of the frozen chunks clanging against the side of the canoe gave hint that we were just a swizzle stick in a cosmic-sized cocktail. Our journey was relatively smooth, though the look on Weldon's face was anything but tranquil.

Approximately two hours after our hasty

departure, still a full day's float from our rendezvous point, we approached a bend in the Wabasca. Ice had lodged in the turn of the river, forming a great dam as the current brought more frozen rafts downstream. Our escape down river was predicated on being able to move with the ice, but now trapped by 20- to 30-foot sheets of ice all around us, we headed toward the stationary wall of jagged, crystalline shards. Weldon revved the Evinrude in an effort to back up and angle the canoe toward shore, but the frozen flows herded us toward the iceberg ahead like a bison being stampeded off a cliff by Apache braves. Weldon's mind was racing to find a solution to our predicament as his eyes jerked quickly back and forth to shore. "Shit," he muttered as we drifted ever-closer to our fate.

Peter, whose canoe was already closer to the river's bank, managed to beach his craft before succumbing to the abominable ice creature before us – a beast that had taken on a sinister life of its own, like a wicked rapids encountered by unsuspecting weekend rafters. Weldon and I remained caught by the current, helpless to change course. 'You wanted adventure,' I thought to myself as we rapidly lost control of the situation.

The canoe rammed the unforgiving ice jam, knocking us forward as we grabbed moose parts to keep from spilling into the river. A moment later, another slab of ice struck us from behind, spinning the canoe crosswise to the current. It was as if we were mice and Mother Nature, with her warped sense of humor, was the fox, toying with us. More and more ice began to build up against the fiberglass and wooden craft, pinning us between the jaws of the flow.

Weldon frantically kicked at the ice that was beginning to buckle the wooden ribs of the canoe while I worked to relieve the pressure of the build-up by futilely chopping at the ice with the blade of a paddle, knowing I couldn't keep pace with the force of the floes being carried by the Wabasca. In the desperate moment when it seemed certain the canoe would be swallowed by the river, taking us along with it, Weldon began leaping up and down. I thought he'd snapped under the stress, but the bouncing raised the bow of the canoe enough to allow the ice to slide under the craft, lifting us out of its crushing grip.

There we sat, on top of an ice jam in the middle of the Wabasca River, 150 miles from the nearest outpost. We still weren't safely on shore, but, exhausted from the frozen karate, we needed a moment to recover before dragging the canoe to the edge of the floe. Once there, we launched the craft again and made it the remaining 40 yards to the river bank, where we built a fire and wondered if this was, indeed, the moose hunt of a lifetime – nearly an abbreviated lifetime.

As we sat in a sober stupor on shore, a search plane buzzed up the river. The pilot tipped the plane's wings to signal that he had spotted us. He radioed back to base that everything was fine, and that we were apparently just running a little behind.

Christmas Valley Corpse

John R. Wright

Nick stopped in for a few days last month. After two years of not seeing each other, we naturally opened a couple bottles of barley pop and settled back to reminisce. Having been acquainted for 25 years, we had plenty of ground to retrace. Working backwards from the recent past, it was only a matter of time and more beer until we arrived at the summer of 1970 and the most memorable event of that season. It started as an ordinary fishing trip, but soon became anything but routine. I knew a fellow from up at the ski hill where I'd worked the previous winter who had a backyard full of horses and didn't mind loaning a couple of them out now and then. We made arrangements for a pair of geldings for a three-day trip and began to assemble our gear.

It was about six miles to Round Lake from the trail head in Christmas Valley, and as we had no pack animal, we figured to travel light. Featherweight down bags, small teapot, G.I. mess kit, and some dehydrated food was about it. That and breakdown fishing rods rounded out our possibles list. Neither Nick nor I now smoke, but we both did then, and his habit was way worse than mine. We talked it over and decided this little expedition might be a good opportunity to give up the noxious weed. We shook on it, saddled up and hit the trail.

Christmas Valley is a narrow, high-sided timber-covered piece of country outside of South Shore, Lake Tahoe, in northern California. The trail to Round Lake starts there and leads you into one of the finest corners of the Sierra Nevadas. We took our time, having only a short ride ahead of us, and stopped often to let the horses blow as we soaked in the view. It was during one of these breaks that Nick began to weaken.

"You didn't happen to accidentally put some smokes in your saddle bags, did you?" The look on his face was a mixture of hope and desperation.

"No," I told him, "that wasn't the deal." He muttered something that sounded suspiciously like "shit." Riding on, Nick and Old Man Nicotine continued to duke it out. I was enjoying it hugely, not being as firmly addicted. I was chuckling to myself when my horse stopped cold in the trail, ears forward and nostrils flared. I was in the lead, and peering ahead I could see nothing. A quarter minute passed, and then there was a flicker in the tress above us that soon materialized as two people afoot, coming down the trail in a hurry.

It was a tall, slender man in his sixties and a woman of similar age. They were dressed to the nines in snappy outdoor togs straight out of L.L. Bean or Eddie Bauer, toting fly rods and wearing fly vests, all spotless and lightly used. They saw us as well, increased their pace, and bore down upon us, puffing, red-faced and flustered.

"Have you seen a forest ranger?" The old man sounded scared.

"Nope," said I. "You're the only folks we've run into this morning." "Well," he blurted, "we were fishing in the creek and found a body." The lady nodded gravely in agreement. "You mean dead?" I asked stupidly. "Yes, he's dead, and I don't mind saying it has ruined our fishing trip." His wife nodded even more vigorously. "That'd sure do it," I agreed.

"We marked the trail opposite the spot in the creek. He's lying in the water. We're going on down to alert the authorities." They started to go around us when Nick inquired, with his most engagingly boyish smile, "Uh, you folks don't happen to have any spare cigarettes, do you?" They recoiled as if they'd been slapped. "I should say not," replied the man. He and his frowning spouse departed in disgust.

"Jesus, Nick," was all I could say. He just

mumbled the fecal word again. Riding up the trail
once more, quiet now, thinking our own thoughts. A
dead guy in the creek. Not your everyday mountain
experience. I'd seen a body or two in funeral homes,
old blue-haired grannies and such, powdered and
peaceful, but a corpse in the back country was something else again. My mental motion-picture studio produced all sorts of grisly scenarios. What circumstances?
Suicide? Accident? Foul play? A broken neck?
Drowned? A bullet hole between the eyes? These were
my thoughts as we rounded a curve in the trail and
saw the marker.

An arrow, made of sticks arranged in a laterally
pointing "V," directed us to the right, into the timber.
I reined in. Nick pulled up beside me and stopped. We
looked at the beckoning sign and then at each other.
"Well," I asked, "what do you think?" Nick gazed off
through the trees. After a pause, he said, "Might as
well check him out." Dismounting and tying the
horses, we eased along gingerly, anxious but in no
hurry. Shortly we could hear the tumbling water, and a
few steps more showed us the creek. Not much to it.
Twenty feet wide, a couple of feet deep, running pretty
fast. No body I could see, just brush, rocks and a log.
A short log. Hold on. That ain't no log. That must be
him. Yeah, that's him. We came up very slowly. It
looked like a man. At least it wore a man's clothes.

Lying on its back, parallel to the current, half under, left arm folded over his face. Merciful good luck there. From the look of that exposed hand, I didn't want to see the face. He'd been there a long time. All winter and spring, as we found out later.

He turned out to be a fugitive. Out of jail on a work release, he'd gone to a party late in the fall, gotten quite loaded on a variety of potent stuff, and elected not to go back to the jug. Striking off cross-country in shirt sleeves and a leather vest, he managed to make about three miles in two feet of crusted snow. At that point (deduced by investigators later) he broke through the thin crust of ice over the running creek, bogged down, and succumbed to hypothermia. Bad luck mixed with stupidity makes for a deadly brew.

We stood there not speaking. The body held no power to sadden or frighten. It was just so much old stuff.

I started to turn away, Nick coming along, but then a flash of devilment took possession of me and I stopped, putting a hand on Nick's sleeve. "He might have a pack of smokes on him. You better go through his pockets, don't you reckon?"

Nick cut me a side glance, looked back at our friend and, with his best bone-dry delivery, drawled, "Aw hell, I expect they're most likely too soggy to light."

Grizzlies and Poodles

John Barsness

Back in the late 1970s I was in Glacier National Park doing a story on the park's bear rangers who patrol the back country keeping an eye on any grizzlies that get too familiar or aggressive with people. Occasionally, if necessary, these rangers tranquilize and move a nuisance bear. After two days around Granite Park Chalet, a young male grizzly that had been hanging around all summer showed up, a bear that various experts had guessed to weigh about 200 pounds. The ranger on duty and I watched him all one afternoon, then that evening trailed him up over Swiftcurrent Pass, finding where he'd cached a mountain goat carcass right next to a popular hiking trail. We backed off immediately, closed the trail, and immediately called headquarters for a bear removal, because the only thing more dangerous than a grizzly on a kill is a mama bear with cubs.

The next day the bear showed up in the same spot. After gnawing on the goat for a while, it started

chasing marmots, turning over rocks with one paw that
later took both of us, using all our strength, to move.
The tranquilizing crew landed and we approached the
bear in subalpine fir that spired over our heads, one
man with the tranquilizer gun and two darts, the two
others with a .44 Magnum handgun and a slug-loaded
pumpgun. After a half hour of "hunting," we eased up
on the bear as it dug after another marmot, and the
dart went into the grizzly's hump. The bear ran off
downhill. We waited five minutes for the drug to take
effect. Then we eased downhill – and couldn't find the
bear. The drug lasts only about half an hour, and after
20 minutes we grew distinctly nervous. After 27 minutes the ranger with the shotgun called, "Here he is!"
We ran over to find the bear lying in a small clearing.
The crew leader poked it with the dart gun, and the
bear turned over and roared, biting at the rifle's
muzzle, though it couldn't rise to its feet. The head
ranger darted it again, and we called in the helicopter
to take it away, into a remote part of the North Fork of
the Flathead River.

But by the time the bear was rolled into a sling
and carried away underneath the copter, it was almost
dark, too late to drop him off safely. The procedure
then, I was told, was to take the bear to an empty
garage that had been reinforced with barred windows
and doors, leave him overnight, then tranquilize him

again in the morning and truck him up the North Fork. We were waiting there the next morning when the truck pulled in, hauling a trailer with a cage made of three-foot-steel culvert. The bear was already awake, and every time anyone came near one of the windows he growled and popped his teeth, the sign of a really mad grizzly. The head ranger eased up to a barred window, carefully shot him again with a dart from a handgun, and again we waited.

Just about then a park policeman drove up and asked what we were doing. When we explained he said, "Oh my God, there's a poodle in there!" It seemed the afternoon before he'd found a white toy poodle wandering one of the campgrounds, obviously separated from its Winnebago. He asked all the campers, but none owned the dog, so he decided to leave it in the bear garage until the owners contacted the park police.

The garage was dark, and even after the bear started to stumble to sleep, we couldn't see well enough to tell if there were bits of white fluff strewn around the interior. Finally the bear was totally out, and three rangers rolled him into the culvert. Then we entered the garage. There was no sign of poodle fur—nothing at all, as a matter of fact, except a pile of old burlap sacks in the corner. We rolled them aside to find the poodle, flat on its belly, a circle of liquid surrounding it, obviously dead. But when the cop touched the little dog, it whimpered. It had found a hiding place during the night, and hadn't even moved to pee.

The bear, by the way, weighed 117 pounds. All grizzlies look bigger than they really are, especially to toy poodles.

Making It Through the Night

Tom Huggler

In late August two friends and I headed into the muskeg tundra country of Ungava, Quebec, in quest of caribou, char, and brook and lake trout. Hearing there were large numbers of willow ptarmigan uninitiated to the upland gun, I packed a young setter, Sherlock, and my 28-gauge. The bird hunting surpassed even my expectations, and after a couple days we were ready to sample the nearby Diana River for spawning trout.

I talked my friends into leaving the comfy base camp at Diana Lake Lodge, which had just opened, and flying 28 miles downriver to a splendid stretch of whitewater. Although the outfitter wasn't yet equipped for outposts, he agreed to loan us a tent and stove that someone had left in camp earlier that summer. On a balmy August afternoon we lifted off with our basic gear and Sherlock. The pilot planned to return the next day to pick us up.

I've spent many nights in many tents (I'm Camping Editor for Outdoor Life magazine), but I wondered now if the high dome-style shelter we unrolled on the suddenly wind-blown tundra would do the job. It took all four of us to hold the flapping beast down while we erected the hoop struts—one of which snapped during assembly—and found rocks big enough to anchor the skip-roping tie-downs. The pilot roared off, and we went fishing.

After an afternoon of fabulous sport and a supper of brook trout baked over coals, we turned in. That's when the wind came up. And then the rain. And then the sleet. The tent, one of those flimsy Korean models you can pick up on special for $79.95, roared all night in the 88-mile-per-hour shearing wind. Sense seeps into your denying brain when you touch the single-walled fabric and your face comes away wet. Full enlightenment occurs when cold water inches down your back. Our three-quarter-length rainfly was all but worthless.

Days later, dawn broke, thin and unsmiling, the fog thick enough to obscure musk oxen across a small lake that heaved whitecaps on the foaming shore. The animals stood with their backs to the blast, which descended from the northeast, backed by the fury of Ungava Bay, with Hudson Bay and the ocean immediately beyond. I wondered if Norse explorers felt as lonely when probing these shores centuries earlier.

Two more poles had shattered during the night. Our tent looked like a shredded airfield wind sock.

One partner, Ed Sutton, and I shored it up as best we could. The other friend, Sigfried Gagnon, tried to make coffee on the sputtering butane stove in our wind tunnel of a shelter. While Sherlock shivered on my sleeping bag, I sipped tepid coffee and dreamed of bacon and eggs back at the lodge. There, a fire crackled in the wood stove. The coffee was hot enough to accept a dollop of cream.

Ed shot me a look as if to say, "This is your adventure, and I don't care for the nightmare." Zipping Sherlock in the tent, we donned chest waders and walked the mile back to the river. Perhaps it was the bad light or the storm itself, but the river was full of silvery char, orange-bellied brook trout, and hungry lakers with big teeth, If we were being punished, we were also being rewarded. About noon, the wind increased–gusting to perhaps 58 mph–and it began to snow. Huge, wet flakes the size of half dollars salted my parka. My hands, under soaked gloves, were frozen, and the cold was seeping through my waders and to my very core. It was time to get out of the river; besides I was worried about my dog.

Hours earlier, Siegfried and I had separated from Ed. Weighted with willow forks holding our still-flopping fish, we staggered over a low esker above camp and spotted Ed, his Blaze-Orange vest a moving fluorescent dot across the tundra. Digging out my binoculars and wiping away the moisture, I could see through the horizontal snowstorm that Ed was stalking a bull caribou. Soon he went to all fours, then to his belly. He shot the animal at 200 yards, then had to wade across a shallow lake to dress it out.

When Ed returned a couple hours later, I noticed the red bandanna around his forehead and feared the worst. "Scope bite," he announced. Lifting the bandanna from the wound, he looked and me and asked, "How bad?" "Not bad enough for a bunch of stitches," I said. "Bad enough so that every time you shave you'll remember this trip." After dressing Ed's wound, I cleaned our catch, some of which Siegfried tried to cook, while Ed rolled more rocks down the hill to secure what was left of our sorry tent. Sherlock was fine, dry on an island of duffel. We used his supper dish to bail 15 pans of water from the inside perimeter of the tent.

When we went to bed, a thin ribbon of orange light to the west promised a better day tomorrow. Although the demonic wind never let up, the stars came out that bitterly cold night, and the northern lights shimmered across the sky like a rising and falling curtain of blue, green and white. Ed slept in his waders. Siegfried wore out the batteries on our flashlights while reading. I zipped Sherlock into my sleeping bag as best I could and, for a little while, stopped shivering.

Dawn broke windless and clear. A fall day with geese calling over the tundra and here and there a gull turning lazy circles in the tame, blue sky. We returned to the river where Ed, an ardent fly fisherman, caught char after char on streamers. Siegfried and I stuck to spinning gear. It was an incredible two hours of fishing: I took an 18-inch brook trout, a three-pound char, and a 10-pound laker on three consecutive casts.

Sherlock, who had gone to the river with us, heard the plane first. Imagine twin surges of emotion, immediate and warring: enormous relief that our adventure was over, deep regret that it had to end so soon.

Lost in My Own Decoys

By Pete McLain

There are some outdoor folks who claim they can find their way on land or water in a dense fog because they have a good sense of direction. I've heard of such people, but I have yet to meet one. Most people find themselves quickly disoriented when surrounded by a heavy fog.

A number of years ago I was hunting waterfowl on Barnegat Bay from a low grass-marsh shooting point that stuck out into the bay. The point, no tiny landmark, was about three miles wide.

There was a light fog before daylight, but I was able to follow the shoreline of the marsh to where I was going to hunt. From the deck of my sneakbox, I set out about two dozen brant, a dozen black ducks, and a few goose decoys, and then pulled the boat up on the salt marsh where the grass was only ten inches high. I removed the decoy racks and spread eel grass and salt hay over the boat to make it blend in with the marsh.

By daybreak I was lying flat on my back, waiting for the opening time. I enjoy hunting alone, as it's a time to think and quietly enjoy the surroundings. I poured a cup of coffee from my vacuum bottle and ate a couple of big chocolate donuts, and was quite comfortable as I waited.

The fog was getting thicker, and I could not see the farthest decoy, which was about 40 yards from my hide. I wasn't too concerned, as I suspected the warm sun rising over the barrier beach would quickly eat up the fog.

By shooting time I could hear some black ducks passing overhead. A flock of brant chattered out in the bay, and occasionally I would hear the honk of a Canada goose. However, the fog was so thick, the waterfowl could not see my decoys even if they passed within 50 yards.

For lack of anything else to do, I lay my head back and tried to take a little nap while waiting for the fog to lift. I had hardly closed my eyes when I heard the sound of wings and the chirp of a goose. When I looked up, two big Canada geese were hanging over my decoys as if they were hooked on a string.

My Browning A-5 dropped both birds in the decoys. One was floating on its back, but the other suffered only a broken wing. He was flopping and swimming out of the decoys, and I made the mistake of not shooting again at the crippled goose.

There is an old waterfowl hunter's saying: "If a goose raises its head, shoot it down." I didn't. The water was only knee-deep, and I thought I could probably chase it down.

I quickly threw the dead goose on the deck of the sneakbox and set off wading into the fog after my crippled bird. It's a rare day when there is no wind on the bay, but this day was flat calm.

Fortunately, I was able to follow the ripples in the wake of the swimming goose. As I got closer, I could hear it try to fly. The bird was swimming just a little more slowly than I was able to run in my chest waders in the two feet of water.

When I closed within 40 yards, I could see the bird, and I shot at it. He was stretched out on the water, and I saw my shot pattern cover the goose, but it didn't stop him.

My heart felt like it was going to jump out of my hunting coat, and sweat was running down my face as I kept up the chase. When I later closed to within 30 yards, the goose raised its head, and I fired my second shell.

The shot ripped the water around the goose, but he never flinched. I had one shell left in the gun and knew if I didn't dispatch the goose, I would never catch up to it.

As I drew closer to the goose, he began to dive and swim under water. This gave me the edge on getting close to him, as I could see the surface ripple where the goose swam under the surface. I pushed him hard, and he surfaced about 20 feet from me – giving me a perfect head and neck shot. The goose was mine.

I picked up the bird, shouldered my gun, and started to walk back toward where I thought my sneakbox and decoys were. As I walked, the water began to get deeper, and before I knew it, I was wading up to my crotch. I realized I must have been walking into the bay and not toward the shallow sand flats.

I altered my course and walked for half an hour and then noticed I was again almost waist deep. I had hunted this area for years and knew there were no channels or deep water within half a mile of my sneakbox.

I admitted I was lost in the fog. I simply didn't know where I was or which way to wade. The goose and gun were getting heavier, and I was getting tired.

I stood still for what seemed like several minutes and listened for any ocean-going boats with fog horns. They would give me an easterly heading.

No fog horns.

I hoped I might hear some other hunter shooting on the marsh where I was hunting.

Not a sound except for sea gulls wandering

42

around in the fog.

I'll admit that I began to feel a little frantic as I walked toward where I thought the marsh was, but always ended up in deeper water. I began to realize that I was walking in big circles rather than in a straight line. How I wished I had a compass so at least I could have walked an easterly bearing.

For two hours that seemed like two days, I waded, always feeling for the shallower water that would mean I was nearing the shoreline. The temptation was to walk in every direction, but I concentrated on trying to walk straight, although I probably didn't.

At one point I considered dropping the goose to save my energy, and admitted to myself, "This is getting serious!" As I waded and thought what to do next, I saw what I thought was a flock of ducks and headed toward them, then decided they were the decoys of a hunter in a sneakbox who was hunting on the marsh.

When I was 30 yards away, I shouted "Hello" several times, but there was no response. I could see the boat and the head of the person sitting in it. I suspected he was sleeping and didn't hear me call.

Moments later, as I was standing in the decoys, I was astounded to see the decoys were mine and the boat was my sneakbox. The "hunter's head" was the goose I had thrown on the boat's deck. My emotions on finding the boat and decoys ranged from confusion,

43

relief, embarrassment, and, eventually, loud laughter at the incident.

One thing I can guarantee: I'll never venture out into the fog again, be it on land or water, without a compass. I'll also quickly dispatch any goose that lifts its head.

Dedicated to Ducks

Don L. Johnson

I've known a lot of fishing fanatics, archery addicts and gung-ho grouse gunners, but when it comes right down to it, I have to say that duck hunters win hands down when it comes to dedication. I'll give you an example.

Some years ago I was invited to join some friends for the waterfowl opener on the Mississippi River, north of La Crosse, Wisconsin. For them it was an annual affair, with the first night of the hunt celebrated with a huge kettle of coot stew and a cold keg of brew.

Enticing as that sounded, I was looking forward to some solo jump-shooting in the Chippewa River bottoms about 50 miles farther north. I promised, however, to show up at their cabin for the stew and to stay to hunt the next morning.

So, on opening day, after bagging a limit of acorn-plump greenheads, I drove down to join the party. The stew was delicious, the beer was refreshing, and the stories were increasingly hilarious as the evening progressed. However, everyone anticipated a good shoot in the morning, so we hit the sack at a reasonable hour.

Three days later, I was cruising along a road flanking the Horicon National Wildlife Refuge, 200 miles to the southeast, when I met a green station wagon which blinked its lights at me. Recognizing the driver as Bob Personius, the refuge manager, I stopped to talk. With Bob was a federal biologist who mentioned that he'd been on the Mississippi over the opening weekend. In the same area, in fact, as I had been.

"I ran into something there that you wouldn't believe," he said.

"Try me," I invited.

"Well, late on the second day of the season I was checking hunters to see what kind of ducks they'd bagged, and also to see if they could identify what they had," he began. "I was just about to leave the landing – it was well after shooting time – when two airboats came up the river."

I nodded, urging him to go on.

"As the hunters landed, I walked down to the shore and asked one of them how they'd done. He answered that they'd done all right, but that they'd also had some bad luck.

"I asked if they'd had motor trouble, if that was

46

why they were late getting in. The guy said, 'No, my brother died.' "

" 'Your brother died? Where is he?' I asked.

"He pointed back to the skiff he was towing.

"Well, there was quite a commotion for a while, trying to get hold of the county coroner, getting transportation for the body and so on. The dead man was in his 50s, I believe. Apparently he'd had a heart attack.

"It wasn't until things quieted down a little that I did a mental double-take. Something seemed strange. I recalled that when I'd helped take the body out of the skiff it was already pretty stiff, and rigor mortis usually sets in three or four hours after death. So I went back and asked the guy when his brother died.

"He said, 'This afternoon.' And then he explained, 'The rest of us decided we might as well wait for the evening flight. He'd have wanted it that way.' "

The Bet

Bill Vaznis

Steve and I rarely get along. In fact, when we were kids we fought like cats and dogs over just about everything. Like the time we slugged it out over who had the best slingshot. It didn't matter that I had hit the most cans off the stone wall, just that Steve's "Ace in the Hole" was made of red rubber, and mine came from an old black inner tube. Dad told us red rubber was supposed to be faster, and therefore Steve's slingshot was better than mine, which is still a crock of bull if you want to know the truth.

Anyway, we're both older now, and although we've stopped blackening each other's eyes, neither one of us has given up on trying to get the best of the other. Take, for example, the one and only time we ever fished the Salmon River together.

I had moved to New York a few years earlier and had been sending back glowing reports of how good the fishing was north of Syracuse. I told Steve twelve- to fifteen-pounders were pretty common, and that he should come up and try to catch one. Well, right off the bat my brother had to tell me he could out-fish me on the river. Me knowing the river like the back of my hand was really no advantage at all, he told me. After all, the wild trout back home were harder to fool than the hatchery-raised steelies I had gotten used to. In fact, he would bet the old rod and reel Dad gave him against my new spinning outfit that I could not out-fish him in my own backyard. Just pick a weekend, he told me. And then he laughed.

Well, come March, Steve and I were on the river. We were trying to scare up a steelie, but the water was high and dirty, and the weather was cold and windy, and by Sunday noon neither one of us had had a fish on, much less felt a good hit. That's when Steve told me it looked like he was going home with my new rig. I didn't beat him, he said. I had to out-fish him to keep my pole, and since we were tied, with no fish apiece, he felt justified taking my new pole and reel home with him.

That's all I needed to hear. I wasn't going to put up with that line of garbage for the next twelve months, so I talked him into going down to a secret spot I knew where a creek emptied into Lake Ontario, to try some bottom fishing.

Maybe I could get a fish there alongside a sunken log, and keep my rod. To tip the scales in my favor, I

lugged two poles down to the mouth of the creek. I
knew Steve's spare rod, a flyrod, was next to useless in
the heavy surf. Too bad, I told him. "You may as well
put Dad's old pole in the back of my truck right now."
He just laughed.

We walked to the end of a stone jetty, tossed out
a couple of nightcrawlers, and then cowered in among
the rocks to get out of the wind. I must have snoozed
off for a few minutes because the next time I looked
over at my new pole it was gone.

Steve, of course, denied having anything to do
with it.

"You never could take care of your gear," he said.
"That's why dad always gave me the good stuff and
you the junk. He knew you would eventually break or
lose anything he gave you." I looked all over for my
pole while Steve just sat there with that stupid grin on
his face. "If you can't find it," he said, "you'll have to
buy me a new one just like it. A bet is bet, and it looks
like I win. Boy, I can't wait to get back home and tell
dad about our trip." I was starting to get a little pissed,
and demanded to know right then and there what he
had done with my pole. Maybe a fish took it, he said.
And then he laughed.

Jesus, I thought. Maybe a fish *did* take my pole!
Steve and I just looked at each other then as if we
had been struck by a runaway ambulance. We both

scrambled for our rods, and then tossed our crawlers out to "my" side of the old log (I didn't tell him one side was better than the other), hoping against hope the pole and the fish that took it were still around.

A few minutes later Steve yelled, "Fish on!" But he said, "He doesn't feel that big. Something's wrong. Can't seem to reel him in." I grabbed his pole and could definitely feel a fish, but it felt like he was snagged on the bottom, too.

I handed the pole back to Steve, and after a few minutes he managed to bring his hook out of the water with a strand of blue monofilament wrapped precariously around the bend. I reached out and grabbed it and started hauling it in hand over hand. Suddenly, the white tip of a Shakespeare Wonder Rod appeared below the surface of the lake, and then the silver- colored bail of a new Mitchell 300. It was my rod! I knelt down near the water and washed the sand from the reel and, Steve acting as my net man, started cranking. A few minutes later Steve flipped a spunky six-pound steelie onto the rocks for me.

We laughed for a while and discussed the impossible odds of what had happened, then headed back to our trucks. It was time for Steve to make the long drive home.

He guessed he won the bet, he told me. After all, if he hadn't snagged my line, I wouldn't have ever known what had happened to my rod, and dad would have thought I was still a klutz. "Besides," he said, "you're lucky that's the only pole I'm taking. Technically, that new Wonder Rod and reel is mine simply because you lost it. And finders are still keepers in my book. I should therefore make you give me your spare rod, too, but I won't. You'll need something for those tame steelies of yours, which I doubt, by the way, you know how to catch." Frankly, I was tired and couldn't keep up with his babble, so I didn't even try to take my new pole out of the back of his truck. Hell, the reel was still full of sand and I'd probably end up buying a new one anyway. Besides, the bastard is two inches taller than me now and outweighs me by twenty pounds. At least I had a fresh trout for dinner.

Steve finished packing his stuff and then quickly hopped into his truck. I was surprised he didn't want to gloat some more. "I'll call you when I get home," he said, and then he gave me a big wave as he drove off.

That's when I saw him laughing in the rearview mirror. I looked back in my truck and realized my little brother had kept the damn fish, too!

Embarrassment Squared

Galen Winter

The ones who got together, created life and then decided how it should operate can, I suppose, be criticized. Really, a better job could have been done. One example of their negligence immediately comes to mind. They arranged for grass to grow and, as a result, need to be mowed during the trout fishing season when a hatch is on.

Another example is their insistence on the immutable rule that every human being must experience one embarrassment so soul-searing that the recollection of it will remain with him until the very end of his days.

Priests and psychologists believe confession is good for us. They claim it keeps us from becoming fearful, anxious and depressed and, in order to compensate therefore, coveting our neighbors ass or violating some other commandment.

(Presumably, if the politicians would all confess, the government of the country would not be so depressing, but such eventuality would fill all the prisons and jails in the land.) Anyway, Grover Thomas must not be depressed because he first swore to me absolute secrecy and then confessed the most embarrassing moment of his life. Here's his story.

Grover was twelve years old and it was the end of November. His dad's deer hunting crew had adopted the practice of inviting the younger generation to their cabin during that final week of the season and introducing them to the joys of deer camp.

It was great fun for the kids. They actually started behaving by November first in order to avoid some sin of omission or commission that would visit upon them the terrible punishment of being barred from the camp.

And when they were in camp, their actions were the marvel of their fathers. Those who weren't already awake in the early morning got up to the shouted advice: "Daylight in the swamp." And unlike back at home, there was no need to yell it even a second time.

Mountains of pancakes and pails of maple syrup disappeared. The youngsters did the dishes without complaint and actually volunteered to fill the wood box and shovel the snow off the path to the outhouse.

In the afternoon they took part in drives. With one adult on each end of a string of pre-teenagers, they were all told: "Watch and remember the direction of the shadows of the trees. That will help you keep going in the same direction. And never, never cross over the tracks of another driver." (Still, two more adults followed them at a discreet distance to make sure no one got lost.) One year they actually chased a deer on a stander. A hundred feet of film was shot, each kid squatting behind the fallen deer, holding a horn in either hand. (And each one planning to tell his less-fortunate non-hunting school chums he had shot it.) They spent evenings in the cabin listening to the "old-timers" tales about the Hoop Snake and the Lumberjack Parrot, the Rockworm and the Sliver Cat. Those evenings were all particularly memorable.

But one of them remains etched in the memory of Grover Thomas. He told me he expected it to be the last thing passing through his mind when he gives it all up and goes to confirm his suspicion that there is no gun control in heaven.

On that one evening, nature (and an overabundance of pancakes) called and demanded action. So Grover took the flashlight and left the cabin to visit the two-holer. A few minutes later, to his consternation, he inadvertently knocked the flashlight off the seat and right down through the adjoining hole.

Panic seized him. If the knowledge of his act ever got abroad, the consequences would be unthinkable. He would embarrass his father. He would prove to be incompetent in the eyes of the other men hunters and never be invited back. And his youthful companions would razz the living daylights out of him.

So he adopted the time-honored program used by all kids whenever they get into trouble: He would say nothing, and if the matter ever came to light, he'd lie about it. Fate, however, was unkind.

He was not back in the cabin for a single minute before one of the adults (who couldn't find the flashlight) went to visit the outhouse. Of course, he saw the light shining up through one of the holes. The cat was out of the bag.

There was no question about it. Grover was clearly the culprit. No defense attorney in the land would do other than enter a plea of guilty and beg the D.A. for a bargain.

In telling the story Grover added: "I'm sure glad my dad had a firm grip on my ankles when I was lowered down to retrieve the flashlight."

A Hunt to Remember

Jim Zumbo

It seemed like a bad dream, but the flames that shot 30 feet out of Doug McKnight's truck were painfully real. We watched helplessly as the vehicle burned furiously in the remote desert. There was nothing we could do. The nearest help was 70 miles away.

"Too bad we don't have a few hotdogs," Doug said, "it's about time for lunch, and we've got a great barbecue fire goin'."

Doug's sense of humor at such a moment was typical, but I wasn't amused.

"You're a weirdo, ol' buddy," I responded. "Your truck is burning to the ground, and you're making jokes."

"Let's cry, then," he said, "or whine or pout. Fact of the matter is, ain't nothin' gonna save that truck, OR this hunt. We might's well save our sanity."

Doug was right. A bit of mirth was no doubt therapeutic. We didn't need any more trauma.

The inferno engulfing the truck represented the

end of a dream hunt. Against terrible odds, I'd drawn a desert bighorn sheep tag in Utah. As North American big game species go, the desert sheep is without a doubt the most elusive and perhaps the most prestigious of all. Only two or three states offer desert sheep hunting, and getting a tag is akin to winning the Publisher's Clearinghouse contest.

Up to now the hunt had been a disappointment. The season lasted 30 days; it would be over soon.

When I learned I'd drawn the tag, my initial reaction was to gather up some good pals and have a proper celebration at the local Elks Lodge. When my head cleared a day or two later, I launched into researching the unit. A buddy had killed a ram there the year before, and he shared information, drawing an "x" on a map where he'd seen a number of good rams, including the one he killed.

"Piece of cake," Paul said about the hunt.

"Lead-pipe cinch, really?" I asked. "No kidding?"

"Duck soup," he responded. "Easy hunt. Park the truck, walk a quarter mile and shoot a ram."

Paul, unfortunately, was not familiar with Zumboism, a term coined by my college classmates. It is the art of doing things wrong, with a great deal of help from Murphy.

I was accompanied on the first five days of the hunt by my good friend the late Ken Heuser of Rifle,

Colorado. Despite serious hip problems, Ken never complained once as we hiked 15 to 20 miles a day across rugged rocky rims in the southern Utah desert. The 100–plus-degree heat didn't help.

As good fortune would have it, or so I thought, we had inadvertently camped close to the only outfitter in the unit. He was a friendly chap and offered suggestions as to where we might hunt. As the days passed and we saw no sheep, I began to suspect that perhaps the outfitter was purposely steering us away from the areas he was hunting with his client. On several occasions, however, we spotted them in the distance, hunting the same general area. When they returned to camp night after night without seeing sheep, as we did, I should have realized that this hunt might not go exactly as expected. The area my buddy had marked with an "X" hadn't held a sheep for months.

Ken and I never found a fresh track. It would have been wonderful to have spotted a ewe, or even a lamb, to indicate the presence of a sheep. Old droppings and weathered tracks were the only signs that sheep had ever been in the area.

The heat was unbearable. Ken and I left camp each day with all the water we could comfortably carry, along with juicy fruits. I recall one occasion when the only liquid I had was in the form of a peach. The fruit was a special reward for getting through the afternoon, and I thought about it every 10 minutes and how luscious the juices would be.

The rattlesnake showed up when I was eating the peach. My brain was so numb from the heat, and I was so desperately involved with the delightful fruit, that I kicked at the snake, which evidently hadn't seen my quiet form and was nonchalantly cruising on by. Ken watched from where he sat, a look of astonishment on his face. The movement of my foot brought the rattler to immediate attention, and I was still unconcerned. Luckily the alarmed reptile crawled away, and as I sat around the campfire that night, I realized that the daytime temperatures were affecting my ability to reason. Any other time, that rattler would have instantly been dealt with in a rather violent fashion, and I wouldn't have been so complacent at its proximity to my foot. And to hell with snake lovers.

Ken and I were dog tired as we packed to leave after the fifth day of hunting. He needed to return to Colorado, and I intended to go home to northern Utah for a couple days, take care of some business, and immediately return to the sheep unit, spending the rest of the season there if necessary.

It didn't quite work out that way. On the drive home, news on the radio told about a Colorado outfitter who was attacked by a grizzly bear. While being terribly mauled by the furious bear, the outfitter managed to stab the bear with a hand-held arrow and kill it.

As editor-at-large for Outdoor Life at the time, my duty was to be on the lookout for great stories. This was a great story, and my boss in New York agreed.

"Get to Colorado, quick," he said, "and get an exclusive on the grizzly attack. I want that story!"

Desert sheep hunting be damned, I thought unhappily, as I sped to the southern Colorado town where the badly injured outfitter was undergoing treatment in a hospital. I was not a happy camper.

Five days later, after being kicked out of the hospital many times by nurses who allowed me to talk to the outfitter only 20 minutes each day, I had my exclusive story. Time was running out on the sheep hunt, however, and it was a matter of putting the pedal to the metal, since it would take another couple days to get home, repack, and drive back down to the sheep unit. The state trooper, unfortunately, was completely disinterested in my excuse as he wrote the speeding ticket. What did he know about sheep hunting, anyway?

Doug McKnight was eager to join me on the remainder of the hunt because he'd hunted the area before and was absolutely wild about sheep hunting. Ken had other commitments and couldn't make it.

Our first mistake was to park my truck at the rim of the desert and take Doug's truck down to the extremely rugged country where we'd hunt.

The term "extremely rugged" doesn't really describe the terrain in the area. Far from it. Rocky outcrops jut up everywhere from the desert floor. Steep slickrock faces and topsy turvy ridges break up the landscape; what roads there are simply defy the imagination.

With Doug's truck loaded with our gear, we crept down the road, and at times I'd have to get out and direct Doug so the tires wouldn't slide us down to oblivion on narrow, twisting turns that were better suited for a mountain bike than a full-sized American-made pickup.

With a great deal of effort and resolve, we made it to the general area we wanted to camp, but we ran out of daylight. By the time we found the spot to pitch our tent, it was dark. Using the truck headlights to illuminate the area, we set up the tent, unloaded our gear, and called it a night.

Unfortunately, we made a mistake, a very profound mistake. When Doug turned the key in the ignition to back the truck away from the tent, the battery was dead, thanks to us using the headlights with the motor not running.

A very dumb move on our part, but the error was

done and couldn't be rectified. Our only option was to hike out to my truck and drive it in to camp. This was not a pleasant task because my truck was at least 24 miles away by our most conservative estimation.

Doug insisted that he walk out, and that I could hunt sheep while he hiked and not lose a day of hunting. That seemed to be a good solution, but I was nonetheless feeling it was a bit unfair for Doug to make the walk. He'd have none of my arguments, however, and was adamant about walking out.

We came up with a guesstimate of how long it would take him to make the trip. A normal human being walks about three miles per hour at a brisk pace, but Doug is not a normal human being. He doesn't walk, he lopes. So figuring three and a half to four miles an hour, he should make it out in six to seven hours, and take another two hours or so to drive my truck in. Giving him an extra hour, a round trip of 10 hours should have done it. Therefore, if he left camp at six a.m., as was the plan, he should be back no later than four.

By four o'clock that afternoon I was about five miles from camp, looking for my first sheep track that wasn't five years old. From a high vantage point I was able to see camp in the distance through my spotting scope, but no sign of Doug or my truck.

Before leaving that morning, I'd tossed an elk

roast, some potatoes, onions, carrots, spices and water in a Dutch oven and buried it in hot coals. I was looking forward to a hearty dinner with Doug that evening, but thoughts of several icy drinks were foremost in my mind. The desert temperatures were still blowtorch hot, just as they had been when I hunted with Ken. At 100–degrees-plus, you think about liquids a lot. A whole lot.

It took me until dark to work my way back to camp. Still no sheep sign, and no Doug at camp. The worrying process was beginning.

As I sat around the campfire, its flames lighting the darkness, my brain conjured all sorts of possibilities. Foremost was the prospect that Doug had suffered a bad migraine and was unable to walk to the truck or drive it back in. He'd told me once that he'd had migraines so bad that he couldn't remember his name.

An hour or so later, I saw an eerie sight. The cliff face opposite camp seemed to suddenly glow in a bizarre light. As soon as it happened, it disappeared. I'm not totally positive that UFO's don't exist, and I was so worked up from worrying about Doug that it didn't take much to get my imagination going in any direction.

Moments later another cliff was lit up by a light. Weird things were going on, and I'd often heard about UFO's using the remote Utah deserts as landing sites.

I'd always dismissed those stories as hogwash, but now, sitting in the quiet, very dark desert with no human within a dozen or more miles, I began to wonder.

When the cliff walls took turns being bathed with lights, it suddenly occurred to me that the phenomenon was caused by the distant headlights of my truck as it weaved its way down the serpentine road.

Fifteen minutes later, Doug drove up. He offered no good excuses for being so late other than he'd spotted some old sheep tracks while walking out and had spent a few hours checking some country higher up. Of course, I never let on that I was a nervous wreck. We ate well that night.

Three more days of intense hunting produced absolutely nothing. In prime spots we'd peer through spotting scopes for hours, but no sheep appeared. Spotting during the heat of the day is a standard way to hunt. It works if there are sheep around. If no sheep are present, you get a whole lot of eyestrain. Frustration is the order of the day.

It was time to go all out, to make a last ditch effort. Doug suggested we try a very remote spot that he was sure no sheep hunters had visited. It was about 25 miles from camp, and a treacherous road led to it. Once there, we intended to bivouac and live in the rocks, drinking water when we found it in tiny seeps and eating dried food that we'd carry in our packs. No tent or sleeping bags; we'd sleep like animals, huddled in whatever sheltered places we could find.

The road was the worst I'd ever seen in a lifetime of hunting. A rocky passage that wound down the side of a mountain, it was built by uranium prospectors 40 years ago. To get down, I walked in front of Doug's truck and guided each tire off boulders as big as washtubs. We inched along, a few feet at a time, bouncing and lurching from one rock to the next.

Finally we made it to the desert floor, but within 10 minutes the truck was trapped in a blowsand wash. The sand was as fine as the type you see on a beach, and we were hopelessly mired. Trying to jack the truck up to put solid material under the tires didn't work either because the sand was too deep, and the jack simply dug in under the truck's weight.

The jack needed a solid base. We hiked about a quarter mile to some rocky ledges, but all we could find was sandstone, which crumbled easily under the weight on the jack.

It suddenly occurred to us that the spare tire would make a perfect base. And it did. But jacking the truck up was just the beginning of the process. We still had to get something under the tires.

Three hours later the truck was free, but only after we'd turned it a full 180 degrees in the sand. We did this by jacking the front of the truck off the ground and pushing it off the jack. Little by little it nosed around, and we had it positioned where it could then be driven out.

Doug finally spun it away from the wash, but we were still on the wrong side. We had to attempt another crossing. Locating a better spot 50 yards up the wash, Doug got a head start, hit the wash and barreled across. At one point the truck was fully in the air, much as you'd see in a cops and robbers chase on TV.

With that major ordeal behind us, we walked over to a small juniper to eat a couple oranges. The tree offered the only shade around.

Suddenly Doug looked over at his truck and made a startling announcement.

"My truck's on fire!"

We ran as hard as we could and saw flames licking along the drive shaft and under the oil pan. Desperately, we grabbed fistfuls of sand to throw on the flames, but we made no headway. Water from our jugs was no help either.

As the flames grew, we realized it was hopeless. Grabbing gear out of the cab, as well as our camp equipment in the pickup's bed, we made several quick trips hauling our possessions away from the burning vehicle. We had no idea why the truck caught fire. Our best guess was that we'd ruptured a fuel line when dig-

ging it out of the wash, and gas spilled on a hot surface
and ignited.

With everything out of the truck, we stood back
and watched helplessly. Deciding that our gear was still
too close to the burning truck, and expecting an explo-
sion when the flames hit the two gas tanks, we carried
everything we owned farther from the truck. A few
minutes later, a small brush fire developed, so we
again moved our gear to another location devoid of
vegetation.

The explosions never came. Instead, the gasoline
burned in a manner we hadn't expected. Twin torches
of flame hissed out of each gas cap, much like an
acetylene torch but much longer. Later I learned from
firefighters that this was typical. Most vehicles that
blow up are pyrotechnic effects of Hollywood techni-
cians. Nonetheless, the rest of the truck burned completely. Glass turned to liquid and dripped down,
burning as it fell away.

When the inferno was at its peak, Doug remembered a handgun in the glove compartment that his
grandfather had given him. It was a goner, along with
other items behind the seat and in the glove box that
we didn't have time to remove. Included in those items
were dozens of rounds of ammo, some .22's and some
high-powered cartridges. They exploded individually
as the heat reached them, along with the truck battery,

which made the most impressive blast of all when it blew up.

It didn't take long before the truck was a pile of molten glass and metal. When it was over, Doug and I walked up to it, but we had nothing to say. I took a few photos of it for insurance purposes, since we doubted that any insurance claims agent would ever get back into that godforsaken place.

Speaking of that remote spot, the next task at hand was to hike the 25 miles back to camp, and return in my truck to haul out all the gear that we'd removed from Doug's truck.

Carrying two jugs of water, we began the journey, starting at dark. Walking steadily, aided by starlight, we made it to camp sometime around two a.m. Too wired to sleep, we broke camp immediately, and by first light we were headed back to the remains of Doug's truck.

I wasn't looking forward to the journey. My truck was brand new, and it was quite possible that the rock-studded road would seriously rearrange the looks of the rig.

It was slow going. The truck bounced and slammed from one rock to another, each tire grabbing or sliding over whatever boulder that was under it.

Upon reaching the bottom, we made several long trips with our gear to my truck, because I wasn't at all willing to attempt crossing the wash. Murphy's law was still very much with us.

The sheep hunt was over. Although we could have given it a try the last couple days of the season, our spirits were broken. I admitted defeat.

* * *

That isn't exactly the end of this story, and it pains me to add this sequel. After we drove out of the desert, the outfitter I'd camped next to during the first week of the hunt had located two legal rams. His client shot one, and the other ran across a draw and laid down in full sight, watching the hunters dressing the first ram. The outfitter sent his guide to look for me, but, of course, I was gone. The guide found an empty camp.

I don't expect to ever draw a desert sheep tag in the U.S. again, and Mexico's sheep hunts are out of reach of my savings account. Nonetheless, the bittersweet memories of that Utah desert will remain with me forever. That, after all, is what hunting is really all about.

The Day This Duck Hunter Didn't Die

By Zack Taylor

It was a day for ducking. Black ducks fly on cold windy days.

This day qualified. Temperatures right at freezing. And the wind came from the northwest in an arctic blast. It was a steady 35 miles an hour. And a northwest wind is like a boxer. It comes at you from various directions. And it calms and gusts. Gusts! Up to 45 miles easy. A howler. A shrieker.

I sat in my blind content. It was a pit blind, cozy and warm.

It was situated on Gulf Point, sealing the bottom of Barnegat Bay. Every duck or brandt, the little sea geese, that came down the bay, would shy from land and swing right over my decoys.

I tended decoys and retrieved birds from my duck boat. Since it is the star of this story, let me tell you about it. I found it awash and wrecked in the river. There were holes in the side, the transom was rotted, and someone had covered the bottom with three-quarter-inch plywood.

I patched the holes, tore off the double bottom, fiberglassed the sweet cedar, and fitted in a new transom. The boat was 16 feet long, round-sided, lap-straked, flat bottomed, planked fore and aft. They call these boats "Jersey Dories." Usually I gunned with a partner, but this howling day I was all one. I used tarred fishermen's lines for my decoy leads. It is tough, cheap, doesn't tangle. I was out in the decoys adjusting them when the prop caught one of the leads. Bang! like that, the shear-pin parted. I was at the mercy of the gale. I was only 40 feet from the shore, but it might as well have been 40 miles.

I kept an anchor always at the ready. It probably saved my life, for it went instantly overboard, caught and turned my dory head to the wind. I was safe for the time being, but the biting cold was already sucking at my strength. And even in the protected lee, the boat was charging back and forth on her anchor line.

Shear pins on outboards are pretty much history. Good riddance! With every new outboard, I always tape a spare pin to the throttle handle. This time the spare was gone. I remembered my partner said he'd broken a pin his last trip. I had failed to replace it.

My situation was grave but not desperate. I considered my options. I could strip and swim to shore.

I'd done some freezing-water swimming before. I could have carried my clothes out of the water. But then I'd be barefoot, and I could hardly swim both my clothes and waders ashore. That meant a barefoot march of about a mile and a half over the marsh to civilization. Would my feet freeze? I didn't want to find out.

I could haul the anchor and let the wind blow me some two miles to the barrier beach. But the seas in the deep water I had to cross would be fierce. Long, rolling breakers. I had an oar aboard. I could use it to keep the boat's stern to the waves. But if I slipped up and the boat turned sideways, it would roll me out. I'd be another dead duck hunter that season.

All this I am thinking as the wind tore at me and the boat fought side to side against the anchor.

It's foolish to think about material things when your life is at stake, but I couldn't help it. I'd land where the wind blew me. What then? How to get the 35 miles back to my car? What about the boat and motor? They'd probably be stolen before I could get back to them. My decoys? My lovely little Parker double shotgun in the blind. How could I get them? Answer: I couldn't.

I had some things going for me, I thought as the wind howled and the boat danced. I had tools aboard. And I had my blind box – assorted nails, wire, staples,

75

used in building and dressing blinds. I pulled off the motor, removed the broken shear pin, and picked out a nail. It couldn't be too thick or I wouldn't be able to break it, but it had to thick enough to hold fast against the bite of the propeller. With a pliers I bent the nail back and forth until it snapped. I put it in place, remounted the motor, and said a short prayer.

Like the obedient slave it was, the motor roared into action on the first pull. With my heart in my mouth, I shifted to forward. The nail held. The boat inched ahead. At dead slow speed I crept back to the blind.

The rest is anti-climactic. The nail drove the boat back to my slip and car. I came home. Was I shook up? Nah! I just went to bed and slept for 13 hours straight.

The Dog Yummy

Pete McLain

I've tried to train and hunt bird dogs and retrievers for a little over 50 years, and I thought I had experience with just about anything that could happen to me while fooling around with man's best friend.

Last November on the opening day of the New Jersey upland game hunting season, however, I experienced an unexpected turn of events.

As usual, I was keyed up for opening day, and my two Brittanies somehow know when hunting starts and were climbing the kennel with excitement.

The sky was clear, but the northwest wind was blowing a gale. My son, Sam, and I were loading my small station wagon with two dog kennels, guns, hunting gear, our lunch, dog water, training collars, beepers, and the usual half-ton of equipment needed for a day of bird shooting.

When the car was loaded, I took Jock out of the kennel on a short leash and tied him to the back bumper of the car while Sam went to get our other Brit, Mark.

My station wagon had two vertical opening rear compartment doors. I opened the larger door and held it open with my hip, as I used my right hand to snap open a heavy steel, spring-loaded latch that locks the smaller door shut. As I opened the latch, a gust of wind blew shut the door I was holding open with my hip, driving my left arm forward and my finger into the latch at the exact instant that I released the latch.

To make a painful story short, the little finger on my left hand was driven into the guillotine-like latch, which neatly amputated the end of my finger just ahead of the first joint. When I looked, the end of the finger was gone, and I was bleeding like a stuck hog.

I raced into the house and wrapped the finger in several layers of paper towels. Sam untied Jock from the back bumper and put him in the kennel, then took me to the emergency room of our local hospital.

The E.R. doctor took a quick look at the finger and sent for a hand surgeon. It took about an hour for this specialist to arrive. When he did, he immediately asked where the end of the finger might be.

Sam went home to look for the lost finger and returned in a half hour with the pronouncement that Jock had eaten it. The doctor, who was not a hunter and appeared not to like dogs, said: "The dog ate it?

Go get that damn dog, and we'll operate and get the finger." I tried to explain how the accident happened and how I had always fed Jock tidbits called "Yummies," which were just about the size of the end of my little finger. When the latch amputated the finger, it fell where the dog was tied, and he must have thought I tossed him a tidbit and gulped it down in his usual manner.

I was firm with the doctor that we were not going to kill my best hunting dog to get the finger back, and he was equally firm with me as he stuck my hand several times with a ferociously long needle, injecting a local anesthetic. He did this to numb the hand so I wouldn't feel the pain when he trimmed the bone and sewed the end of the finger into a neat little stump.

Several times I heard him say, "The dog ate the finger?" When the local anesthetic wore off, I suffered some pain, but wore a special finger guard to prevent bumping the bandaged stub.

When I wrote a newspaper column on this adventure, the editor called and asked: " What are you trying to do, freak out the readers?" The remainder of that season I hunted with a mitten on my left hand and cut the thumb and forefinger out so I could work the gun's safety and pull the trigger. During the cold weather in December and January, I inserted in the mitten one of those little chemical packets that generates heat, to keep the cold air off the sensitive end of the finger.

You never realize how important the little finger is in your daily routine. I don't know how many drinking glasses have fallen through my left hand. Most people support a glass by curling the little finger under it. It's usual when you lose an appendage to think it's still there. So glasses simply fall through my grip, and everyone thinks that I have had one too many.

The real annoying parts about the dog eating my little finger was the $1,600 surgeon's bill, and every time Jock looks at my hand, he sits up and begs.

World Record Bass Survives Cocaine Bust

George H. Harrison

"Anyone want to catch a world record fish today?" Buck Rogers asked our group of intrepid outdoor writers at El Dorado Lodge on Colombia's Vaupes River. I was there to photograph and report on the wildlife in the Amazon jungle, not to catch trophy fish. But several of the group were among America's foremost fishermen, and everyone was listening.

"The peacock bass is being listed this year for the first time in the records of the International Game Fish Association (IGFA), and any fish we catch could be a world record," Buck continued. "Who has 8-pound-test, 6-pound-test and 4-pound-test line?" he asked. "I have 4-pound test on a Daiwa Minicast rod," I spoke up. Someone chuckled.

"Good, Harrison, you catch a world record peacock on 4-pound-test line and the rest of us will fish with other line strengths," Buck responded.

So, I fished the Vaupes on January 8, 1980, with

my little Minicast equipment and 4-pound-test line,
hoping that I would catch something, anything. The
day before, I had fished with Sports Afield angling
editor Homer Circle who reeled in a 13-pound peacock bass on 14-pound-test line. "That would have
been a world record," I reminded Homer later. "Yeah,
maybe, but I'm past the time in my life when keeping
a trophy fish gives me a thrill," Homer explained.

"Well, I haven't quite passed that point," I
responded sheepishly. That's because I had never
caught a trophy fish, and I certainly didn't expect to
catch one there with my bluegill outfit. Besides, I had
come on the trip to experience the wildlife – such
bizarre creatures as anaconda, jaguar, capybara, fruit
bats, and tapir. The birds were incredible: parrots and
parakeets chattered in flocks above the jungle canopy;
long-tailed hummingbirds zipped from one orchid to
another; and heavy-billed toucans fed on papaya.
These were the things that occupied my thoughts, even
while I fished for peacock bass from a dugout canoe in
the Vaupes.

Imagine my shock when a big fish took my
Wisconsin-made white jig and headed for the bottom.
The little Minicast rod immediately bent into a question mark, and the 4-pound-test Trilene was as tight as
a violin string. What do I do now?

Had it not been for my companion, Dan Klepper,

outdoor editor of the San Antonio Express-News, I surely would have lost that fish. Dan coached me through the full 20 minutes it took to land it. We didn't even see the fish for the first 10 minutes. After that, each of the seven times the big peacock came to the surface, the fish took a look at us and made another sizzling run to the snag-infested bottom. Each time, I was certain it would be the last time I would see that fish.

On the eighth rise, our Colombian guide, Alirio Mora, stretched out his arm with the net as far as he could reach and bagged it!

My yell of triumph resounded so far into the jungle that it was answered by a troop of howler monkeys a mile away.

The fish weighed 12-1/2 pounds on my field scale and appeared destined to be a world record, if only I could get it back to the U.S. to have it properly recorded. Little did I know that catching the fish would be easy compared to the danger that lay ahead.

The next morning we broke camp and motor-boated up the Vaupes to the jungle village of Miraflores, where a DC3 would pick us up on the dirt landing strip that was also the main street of the village. As we approached the village dock, we could see that something very strange was in progress. Para-military gunmen, armed to the teeth and dressed in white

T-shirts with the letters "DAS" inscribed on their fronts, awaited us. We had arrived in the middle of a cocaine raid, and everyone in the village was under armed guard while their houses were searched for drugs. You can image the delight of the raiders when they spotted a boatload of "gringos" arriving at the dock. Had they found the cocaine motherlode or what?

Their rifles and pistols aimed at us, we were ordered to put our hands on our heads and march to the airstrip. "Leave your luggage in the boat," we were told in Spanish. While we stood the prescribed 10 meters apart on the airstrip for two hours in 90-plus-degree midday heat, the drug squad opened each of our bags and looked for the cocaine they were convinced we were trying to smuggle out of the country.

I could see my large green dufflebag, containing the hoped-to-be-world-record peacock bass, piled up in the heat with the rest of the luggage to be inspected. I was sure that when they found the carefully wrapped frozen fish, they would know that the drugs were hidden inside it.

Meanwhile the heat began to take its toll. Field and Stream angling editor Ed Zern had not been feeling well that morning, and being forced to stand in the heat for two hours made him feel even worse. He needed a toilet, and he needed it badly. But the raiding party refused to let him find relief. "No. You stay there," ordered a sneering young guard.

At that moment, three quick shots rattled out of his automatic rifle, passed between Zern and me, and perforated a tin shack on the other side of the runway. Everyone hit the ground.

The kid holding the smoking rifle grinned in embarrassment. His commanding officer approached and questioned him. He explained that it was a mistake; he had been adjusting the ammunition cartridge while his finger was on the trigger, and the bullets had fired.

The commander shouted something at him, ordered him away, and replaced him with another guard.

But this near-tragic incident was as much as we were willing to tolerate. Tom King, who was then vice-president of Braniff International and a host for the trip, summoned the commander for a man-to-man chat in fluent Spanish. This broke the ice, and we were allowed to retire to the shade of the nearby cantina. Zern found a toilet.

I do believe that the bizarre shooting incident by the young guard distracted the forces enough to cause them to overlook several pieces of luggage, one of which was my dufflebag containing the fish.

We faced further delay as our pick-up plane was

diverted from landing several times while more military forces landed. Apparently a sweep of the jungle was underway, and by the time we were finally allowed to leave, there were hundreds of troops on the ground.

Some 96 hours later, I eased the thawed peacock bass onto the official scale of the IGFA in Ft. Lauderdale, Florida. The fish officially weighed-in at 12-1/4 pounds, was 29-1/2 inches long, and had a girth of 19 inches (plenty of room to hide drugs). It was listed as the 4-pound test line world record for peacock bass for more than 10 years, until someone bettered it in Venezuela.

"Old Peacaine" still hangs on my office wall and gives me no end of memories about that remarkable day in the Amazon jungle of Colombia, when a world record bass survived a cocaine raid.

Tree-Swatting

Dave Duffey

Maybe they're still running it. It's been a few years since I was there. But the Ruffed Grouse Society used to conduct a real fun hunt for partridge and woodcock up in northern Minnesota, based out of Grand Rapids, if I remember right.

Teams made up of two hunters and a dog were spread through excellent bird cover in that vicinity, their bags were brought in for checking and study by a Society game biologist, evening seminars were conducted on such things as grouse and timber management, dog training, and shotgunning, and so forth.

Being invited to participate (and to conduct a seminar on grouse and woodcock dogs), I was to discover that there was some real good partridge and 'doodle hunting in that sector of Minnesota and a lot of nice people who were serious hunters. But in any gathering you find yourself encountering some "strange" people; the basis for their "strangeness" being that they have a viewpoint different from your own.

As a small-town kid growing up in the Depression
years, my perspective on partridge (ruffed grouse) was
that they were pretty stupid birds, "woods chickens" to
be potted for meat, whether ground-swatting them with
a shotgun when they were picking grit and greens on
logging roads or picking them off popple boughs with
a .22 rifle after a dog flushed them up the tree.

No matter how sophisticated a sportsman
becomes, his boyhood clings to him. A man can
become defensive when he encounters "different"
people whose procedures and fetishes jar long-dormant
animosities.

As the rules of the hunt were being explained at
the Friday afternoon pre-hunt gathering, it became
obvious that in all likelihood a Wisconsin country boy
like me might be excoriated, then buried in self-right-
eous bullshit, however pure and sanitized the burial
mound was.

It was obvious that a considerable portion of the
hunters in attendance were there to venerate, rather
than ventilate, *Bonasa umbellus* and *Philohela minor*. I
wouldn't have been at all surprised to hear some of
them refer to hunting as "the art of venery."

So, after they laid down the rules about no
ground-swatting and no shooting birds out of trees, I
thought to lighten things up by rising to my feet and,
in an incredulous tone, ask: "You mean we got to shoot

'em on the fly for the birds to count? Hell, that's a waste of shells. Can I get my entry fee back?" I had expected at least a chuckle, if not laughter. My little joke, however, evoked nary a snicker. What smiles there were, for the most part, were forced, frozen, not even condescending or polite.

"If you want to see me about a refund, after we finish, come up . . ." I interrupted the chairman . . . "Aw, hell! Never mind. I'm still in." With that, the chairman, with apparent trepidation, told the gathered hunters that I'd be conducting the dog training seminar scheduled to begin when this meeting recessed.

I turned to my long-time friend and hunting partner Jerry Kavaney and said: "We're here to hunt and have fun. But this is war – the Paddies against the aristocrats. We'll have some more fun with these guys at the seminar." Then, with a few minutes to spare between adjournment of the rules meeting and the beginning of the dog training session, we again repaired to the Holiday Inn bar to instigate another fire-fight in the campaign both of us were waging to convince our doctors that sour mash bourbon and water helps victims of arteriosclerosis.

Because an evening, indoor meeting ruled out any hands-on demonstrations, I explained to the crowd that filled the conference room that this would be a question-and-answer training seminar . . . anything they wanted to know about gun dogs but had been afraid to ask, I'd try to answer.

The first gentleman on his feet was the epitome of a properly turned-out eastern Anglophile, a serious practitioner of the art of upland game shooting, from wool hat (replete with grouse feathers and field trial pins) to sort of chukka-style high shoes like those L.L. Bean used to call Maine Guide Shoes. His breeches were tucked into knee-high wool socks, and his tattersall shirt was topped with an Ascot.

Properly ruddy face, breaking into a quizzical smile, he asked: "Mr. Duffey. What, in your opinion, is the prime requisite for a perfect grouse dog?"

"Voice!"

That single word, emphatically delivered, actually made the questioner blink. His face went blank for a moment and, as I started to take advantage of the burial-vault silence in the room, he recovered and managed to croak: "Voice?"

"Hell yes, voice! Look, when you're out hunting and your dog runs off – lookin' for birds if you're lucky and there aren't any deer around for him to chase – when he finds those birds, how in hell are you going to find him unless he's got a far-carrying bark so you can get to him and shoot the bird out of the tree? No matter how good a bird-treer the dog is, if he's deficient in voice, you aren't going to kill many birds."

It was fortunate that there were several others in the audience with whom I had more than a nodding acquaintance. They chimed in, convincing the others that what I had said was whimsical and uproariously funny. Everyone relaxed and we got down to serious business. But I could tell that the prim and proper among the crowd remained more than a bit skeptical of any answers given to the questions.

I got my come-uppance for "country-boying" the sophisticated the next day. Each team was assigned a guide-scorekeeper to keep things honest, jotting down finds, hits, misses, retrieves by the dog, and so forth. Our escort was a quiet, unobtrusive logger who pretty much kept out of the shooters' way but missed very little of the action or verbal by-play.

So as we drove out to the hunting area and parked in a borrow-pit off a logging road, I made it a point to give sotto-voice instructions to Kavaney regarding how we'd conduct the hunt. Like: When the dogs barked treed, how he should distract or engage the scorekeeper's attention so I could go to the dog, holler "there it goes" and shoot the sitting bird out of the tree without being observed by our supervisor . . . a nd so on and so on . . . all playing around with finding ways to ostensibly follow the rules while hunting the way we were accustomed . . . pot shooting birds the dogs treed, ground swatting those they didn't, and so on and so on.

Little did I realize how this joking would backfire.

I had hauled along four dogs, if I remember right: a Springer, a Labrador, and a couple of Pointers. I'd planned to run the Springer and Lab as brace and pair up the Pointers. But the rules of the hunt specified one dog at a time for each two-man team.

Because the dog power at this gathering leaned heavily to traditional English Setters and practical Brittanies, partly to demonstrate how far removed I was from this mainstream, I opted to put the Springer, Duff's Pestilence, into the cover first. Spaniels and retrievers are great grouse and woodcock producers and recoverers. In my misspent lifetime I very well may have killed more game over flushing dogs than I have over pointers.

As we hiked briskly up the tote road to get to a likely looking popple stand we'd passed driving in, Pest worked as a spaniel on a partridge hunt ought to: criss-crossing the road to poke into the cover on either side, responding to occasional whistle beeps and hand signals to check out by-passed cover clumps.

But we hadn't progressed 100 yards when it happened. I swear to you that this dog had never in his life done this before, and he'd been responsible for providing shots at literally hundreds of game birds representing most of the species found in North America.

92

As he ducked into the cover on the right of the trail ahead of us, a late-migrating robin popped out and flitted up into a bush. Pest followed it out, spotted it, sat under the bush, then reared back and barked at it. When he danced around, barking, the robin flew.

Loathe to let this lie (and ever mindful of the dog trainer's axiom to claim that anything your dog does is just what you trained him to do), I turned to the guide and said: "Little son-of-a-bitch got out of that bush before I could get the gun up. But if Pest puts him out again, I'll be ready for him. Cajuns down in Louisiana showed me how good robins are to eat."

When we got back to the lodging place that night, I have no idea what the scorekeeper-guide told the hunt officials, but it probably began: "You know this guy you thought was joking about his dog barking at treed birds and shooting the birds out of the tree . . . well, you aren't going to believe it, but . . ." The annual Ruffed Grouse Society Ruffed Grouse and Woodcock Hunt was the most fun shindig to which I was never re-invited.

Hellacious Moose
(or The Moose Hunt From Hell)

Chris Dorsey

[Author's note: Names have been changed to protect
the guilty.]

As bush plane landings go, this was a fairly good
one—just the usual burps and gurgles as the plane met
the waves and Fred's breakfast began a tug of war
between his throat and stomach.

"Nice landing," I shouted over the Otter's still-
roaring engine.

"Any landing you can walk away from is a good
landing," answered the pilot, a grizzled old salt whose
breath hinted of whiskey and whose bloodshot eyes
looked like half-developed egg embryos.

The pilot throttled the plane down a narrow
channel where Fred, whose digestive system was
beginning to settle, had built a crude camp from which
moose hunting forays could be launched. I was on
assignment for a national sporting magazine to relate

the drama of a north woods moose hunt and was
happy to have the work. Two hunters from Minnesota
were already in the camp along with two Cree guides.
Since there was no radio communication from the
hunters, we hoped they'd be waiting for us at the designated beach as we arrived exactly on the predeter-
mined day of pick up. Being transported on time in the
far north by a bush plane is a rare event—something on
the order of being struck by a meteorite.

As we rounded the final bend with a degree of
trepidation, the encampment came into view: two
hunters, two guides, and three canvas tents still standing—success! As we got closer to the beach, the faces
on the Indians appeared noticeably dour, and the two
hunters sported stares reminiscent of a rabid Charles
Manson. Fred opened the door of the plane and faced
the verbal barrage of two miffed hunters who had
plenty of time to ponder the inadequacies of the hunting operation.

"Goddamnit Fred, the boat motors didn't work all
week. We ran out of bread two days into the hunt.
Your guide cut his wrist [accidentally] with a fillet knife
and you didn't even have a Band-Aid in camp! What
the hell . . ."

The two hunters took turns as if their performance had been rehearsed.

"Goddamnit Fred, there aren't any moose around

here. We had to paddle around the whole lake. You know how big the swells get on this lake? You were supposed to pick us up two days ago. These fishing rods are pieces of shit. Goddamnit Fred . . ."

I looked at Fred as he teetered on one of the plane's pontoons – his belly was starting to gurgle again.

"You didn't tell me your first name was Goddamnit," I said in a pathetic attempt at levity that I hoped might prevent a homicide in the bush.

"Let's get the hell out of here," the two hunters said in unison as they began loading the plane with their belongings.

I'm not one to readily recognize an omen, but this message was as subtle as a moose standing on my chest. My mind raced for an excuse to stay on the plane and forget the magazine assignment.

"C'mon Chris, we'll show 'em how to hunt moose," said Fred, counting on me to rescue the moment.

I looked at the pilot and said, "I've got two bottles of Chivas in here . . . if you make it back in five days they're yours."

The guides finished loading the hunters' gear and climbed into the plane to disembark for civilization – such as it is in the Canadian north woods.

"Where the hell do you think you're going?" says

Fred to Bushwhacker, the nickname of one of the guides whose wrist is showing signs of infection after the fillet knife incident.

"Home, my wife's expecting me."

"The hell you are," said Fred, "you're supposed to guide this hunt, remember. You get on that plane and you'll never guide in this province again."

I don't know if Bushwhacker took Fred's comments as a threat or a promise, but he nevertheless tossed his bag off the plane and surrendered his services to us for the next five days, or until death do us part.

There I was, sent 200 miles from the nearest outpost to do a story on a guide and outfitter who wouldn't speak to each other. Five days of bliss you never read about in the sporting press. The silence didn't last long as Bushwhacker had gotten one of the boat motors to work and we headed off to the other side of the lake to see if we couldn't grunt up a moose before sundown. That gave Fred ample time to organize camp and plot Bushwhacker's murder. Sunset came and there was no sign of moose, just the stillness of a northern lake whose waters turned to mercury before imminent freeze up in another few weeks.

"Let's give it a shot in the morning," I said, figuring there wasn't enough light left to see a moose — or, for that matter, a floating log in our path during the boat ride back.

"This is just when the hunting gets good," said Bushwhacker, taking a drag off one of his hand rolled smokes, "the moon will be out soon and you'll have plenty of shooting light then."

"My night vision isn't worth a damn . . . besides, Fred is expecting us for dinner," I said, hoping Bushwhacker might see the humor in the comment. He didn't.

The boat ride back was a white-knuckle affair as Bushwhacker did his best to see if the boat couldn't skip across the water like a flat stone flung by Nolan Ryan. My knees bounced to my chin as we bottomed out over each swell in what amounted to a hemorrhoidal maneuver. I'd have killed Bushwhacker myself, save for the fact that we were in the midst of a four mile long lake in near darkness, and I'm not particularly adept at navigating unfamiliar lakes by starlight.

Back at camp, Fred finished frying trout fillets that, at that point, were the highlights of the experience. We sat and ate in utter silence around the fire while Fred and Bushwhacker still wouldn't exchange thoughts – not even bad ones. Four more days and counting.

Before turning out the lantern for the night, Bushwhacker went to the beach to make sure the boat would be ready for the morning hunting. His departure gave Fred the opportunity to vent his thoughts on his chief guide.

"Don't turn your back on that son of a bitch, he's just like every other Indian, you can't trust him to do anything right."

There you have it, one goddamnit, one son of a bitch, and one writer in camp – some might say the three of us were meant for each other. The harmony continued for the duration of the hunt as the silence was beginning to ring like a form of tinnitus in my ears.

The last night in camp, after not having seen a hint of a moose, Fred and Bushwhacker decided to make their peace, knowing that their return to the same small town dictated a certain degree of civility. To celebrate the moment, Bushwhacker pulled a small plastic bag from his backpack and poured a little pile of hashish onto a tin plate. He and Fred took turns puffing smoke and soon the hard feelings melted away along with their brain cells. At that point, Fred turned to me and asked, "Think you can do a good story about this hunt?"

"Yep . . . someday."

You'll Never Boat That Shark

John Barsness

We were off the shore of Andros Island in the Bahamas, my Florida friend Jim Conley and I, deep-jigging a reef for whatever came along. Our two guides were Felix, a tall strong man of about 40 who preached when he wasn't guiding, and Clifton, a short, quiet young man just out of high school, still learning the guiding trade. We'd already caught some barracuda when Jim put the hook of his jig into something big that just stayed down. "I think it's a big shark," Jim said, leaning back on the 50-pound line.

Felix looked into the water, listening to the drag ease out. "You'll never boat that shark. Not on that line, no sah." That was the wrong thing to say. Jim is one of those Florida backwoodsmen who's about as predatory as a ten-foot alligator. Once he actually caught one on a surface lure on his trolling tackle in the canal behind his Orlando home, and was about to tie it to a tree when, as he puts it, his "goddamn lawyer neighbor came up and told me it was illegal." The

gator went for the lawyer and broke off. The lawyer
went for his backyard gate and hasn't spoken to Jim
since.

"Wanna bet?" Jim said to Felix, tight-lipped.
Ordinarily he'd have just broken the big fish off and
tried for something more manageable on such tackle,
but you do not challenge Jim.

Forty-five minutes later Jim was drenched with
sweat and we could see occasional flashes of something
bigger than a ten-foot alligator in the water below the
boat. "Felix, you and Clifton each get a gaff" – Jim
nodded at the two hand gaffs – "and stick him on
either side of his head. Then we'll tie a rope to his tail,
drag him around backwards and drown 'im!" Felix was
duty bound to try, but Clifton looked rather doubtful.
Five minutes later the shark was alongside the boat
and Jim leaned back, red faced and arm weary. The
sharks' head came up next to the gunwale and it
opened its jaws. Felix stuck him, but Clifton leaped
completely over the control panel of the boat, ending
up leaning as far as he could over the opposite gunwale. The shark gave two shakes of its head and shook
off Felix. The line popped, and the shark sank out of
sight.

Nothing happened. Jim stood there, drained.
Felix stood there, astonished. I stood in the bow, where

I'd been photographing the whole scene. Finally, Clifton's head showed above the controls, and Jim waved him over. "Come on, kid. Let's catch another one." And even Clifton managed a laugh.

One Small Leap

George Laycock

Some years ago, on an assignment for *Audubon* magazine, I was invited to accompany the inspection crew of wildlife biologists that the U.S. Fish and Wildlife Service sent out once a year into the remote leeward islands of the Hawaiian Islands National Wildlife Refuge. This was a rare invitation to see wildlife islands that few people were allowed to visit.

These little islands lie in a thousand-mile-long chain reaching out northwestward into the Pacific–beyond Hawaii's well known main islands–all the way to Midway. Every hundred miles or so there is one of these remnants of long-extinct volcanoes. Our crew of five would make the trip aboard the USCG Cutter Buttonwood. The Coast Guard promised to put the "bird people," as they called us, ashore on the various islands for periods ranging from half a day to three days.

Many of these islands have been worn by wave and weather to flat little bits of land lying close to sea

level, but a few rise precipitously out of the Pacific.
One I will always remember is Necker Island, which
covers only 45 acres but rises 278 feet above the
ocean in sheer, rocky cliffs.

Our first problem here was getting onto the island
and climbing to the top of the jagged cliffs to census
the nesting sea birds. The Coast Guard took us in close
to the cliffs in their rubber raft and, with the help of a
small outboard motor, held the raft alongside while
each new wave lifted it up to the black lava shelf
where, one at a time, we scrambled off onto the
narrow ledge made slippery with saltwater spray.

From this perch we worked our way to the top.
The thousands of sea birds, unaccustomed to mam-
malian predators, were trusting enough to sit securely
on their ground-level nests, allowing us to move
among them, counting and photographing. We kept
busy until nearly five o'clock in the afternoon, when
the Coast Guard was scheduled to rescue us.

Throughout the day the rising winds drove dark,
rolling waves steadily higher against the cliffs.
Occasionally I thought about the coming departure,
but I relegated any doubts to the back of my mind.

By five o'clock the five of us were assembled
again on the cliff top. We saw the raft leave the
Buttonwood a mile distant and head straight for us
until it edged alongside Necker Island. Soon each wave

106

was lifting the raft higher than the previous one had, and seawater now sloshed in over the shelf and around our boots, promising to suck us into the ocean. The receding waves dragged four small packs of equipment out into the deep while we scrambled farther up the rocks.

Timing was critical when entering the raft. There came a fleeting instant when each incoming wave peaked and, in that brief moment while the raft hesitated, one of us would step aboard and ride it back down into the trough. If a person missed the boat, he would be at the mercy of the rocks and waves. Soon I was next in line.

I carried a large aluminum camera case, heavy with Hasselblads, and that may be why I hesitated an instant too long. As the raft began its descent, someone behind me yelled above the noise of the turbulent sea, "Get in!"

Cameras in hand, I launched myself into the air out over the rolling waves. As the raft slid into the trough below me, I landed splayed out squarely in the middle of it, rejoicing in the knowledge that, although my timing was off, my aim was true.

Fly Me to the Tree

Don L. Johnson

Virtually anyone who's spent much time in the far north has some keen recollections of times spent with bush pilots. Bush planes are like magic carpets for those who want quick conveyance to remote regions. They whisk us away from turmoil and set us down in silent surroundings where everything is still in its proper place, where the fish are huge and hungry, where massive moose wade along the shores. However, sometimes it's the flight itself that is the most memorable part of the trip.

I usually feel safer in a small plane with an experienced bush pilot at the controls than I do in freeway traffic. However, in more than 30 years of roamings as an outdoor writer, I've had a few hair-raising times in airplanes.

Like the time in 1969 when photographer Jim Meyer and I went up to the Northwest Territories. I'd been assigned to write a series of stories about the fishing on and around Great Bear Lake, while Jim was to be shooting a movie. We'd heard about a spectacular spawning run of arctic char in the Tree River and we especially wanted to get there. Although we knew that the weather would be chancy, we opted to go in early September in hopes of hitting the peak of that run.

A charter plane landed us at Great Bear Lake, on a gravel strip which had served a small, recently abandoned military base. Some canny entrepreneurs had just bought the facilities and turned them into a fishing camp.

We were met by bad weather — wet, cold and windy — but made good use of our time while waiting to fly on to the Tree. Great Bear Lake then was virtually a virgin fishery. Except for some small-scale mining and the military base, there had been little development around the huge lake. Also, it was too remote to make commercial netting feasible. So, for some years, sport fishing camps proliferated and prospered there.

We had arrived at the beginning of that bonanza. We caught and filmed giant lake trout and also fished some tributaries for northern pike and grayling. However, we fretted more each day. The Tree River was still 250 miles away and time was short. Our hopes hung on Ernie Boffa, the only bush pilot still around those parts so late in the season.

Ernie was 60 years old then and already a legend

in the far north. As impetuous as I was in those days, I knew better than to argue with him about when to fly. Arctic weather is especially uncertain in autumn, and there were no observers to the north to advise us on conditions there.

Finally, after three days of stormy skies, we awoke to see the sun beaming through the window. Dressing hurriedly, we scrambled down to the dock and found Ernie topping off his gas tanks, cautiously straining the fuel through a chamois skin to absorb any water it might hold.

"It's clearing to the north, so we'll try it, but don't dally!" he said.

We didn't. We wolfed some breakfast and grabbed a few candy bars for lunch while Ernie loaded our fishing tackle and photo equipment into his Cessna 180 floatplane.

Another angler, Earl Derby, of Milwaukee, decided to join us. Because he was the millionth person to send a vacation inquiry to Canada's tourism bureau, Earl had won a trip to anywhere he wished to go in Canada. He had flown to Great Bear with us, and now chose to go to the Tree. So, with Earl and Jim buckled up in the rear seats and me beside him, Ernie cranked up the Cessna and took off.

Minutes later, as Lake Dumas passed 4,000 feet below us, the plane seemed to go over a bump. Ernie had just nudged the controls. "We just crossed the Arctic Circle," he explained with a grin. The horizon ahead showed only a few cottony clouds. We were all exultant about the weather.

It was still clear when we crossed the Coppermine River more than an hour later. I remember how the limestone cliffs along its banks were shining in the sun. However, low, dirty-looking clouds suddenly loomed ahead, and before long we were in them. Ernie descended to 1,500 feet, trying to keep the ground in view, but the rough-looking tundra was soon obscured by swirling snow. Ernie nosed the plane lower, gripping the controls grimly as the air became increasingly turbulent.

We emerged from that snowstorm maybe 15 minutes later, but our problems weren't over. We were enveloped in a dense, freezing fog. I watched tight-lipped as a glaze began forming on the wings. Ernie was quiet, but I knew from his actions that the plane was responding poorly. Ice was building on the propeller too, and pieces of it were being thrown from the whirling blades. The plane shuddered with vibrations from the now-unbalanced propeller. I stared at the altimeter. The needle didn't have much farther to go.

Then, not far below the pontoons, I could see tossing waves. To me, they were not a welcome sight. Ditching in the Arctic Ocean was far down on my list of things to do that day. Still, Ernie held his course northward, flying low, heading farther out to sea.

That canny old bush pilot knew what he was doing. Warmer air, rising from the water, began to thaw the ice from the plane. The fog thinned too. Presently we turned eastward and skirted the edge of the departing fog bank until glimpses of the shoreline appeared.

"I know where we are," Ernie said finally. And we continued to the mouth of the Tree.

The rest of the day was anticlimactic, but no less memorable. As we taxied shoreward, a parka-clad Eskimo, face framed with fur, paddled a kayak out to meet us. It was a scene right out of my grade-school geography book. Jim was impressed too. "Jeez!" he muttered, "Are we ever NORTH!" Some Eskimo families had a summer camp near the mouth of the river. They were gathering large numbers of fish and seals to feed their sled dogs during the long winter. (This was long before snowmobiles began to replace dog sleds in those latitudes).

We hitched a boat ride upriver with an Eskimo who was tending gill nets, which had been set at many points upstream. Where they had already been emptied, the river banks were heaped with arctic char, some gleaming silver; others glowing with color, their red-orange sides beaming like neon signs. Many were still flopping, spewing golden spawn on the gravel. They were huge. Some doubtless would have been new records if taken on hook and line.

We had trouble finding a decent place to fish because of all those nets, but we finally clambered ashore about a mile upstream and began casting. I tried a saltwater flyrod for a while. The action was fantastic, but trying to hold those fish in the roiling currents was almost impossible. I then switched to a stout spinning rig and promptly had a 15-pound-test line snapped like store string. We caught and released some 10- to 12-pounders and kept one which weighed about 16. Some of those we lost were awesomely bigger.

After three hours we were weary, our tackle was battered, and Jim had all the movie footage he needed. Also, the sky was looking ominous again. Ernie, who had stayed with his plane, was glad to see us return. We raced another squall back to Great Bear Lake and landed in a buffeting wind. The weather turned nasty again soon after we tied up.

While we were unloading our gear from the bouncing plane, someone mentioned that it was Labor Day back home.

"Well, at least we took the National Safety Council's advice and stayed off the highways today," Jim said.

Everyone laughed. Except Ernie.

That Reminds Me of the One . . .

Steve Smith

I thought I'd tell about the time on a grouse hunt that not only did I manage to get on the dry end of the line, Tom Petrie and his brother Chuck were down in the swamp—mud and knee-deep water—pushing the grouse out over Our Hero. I was walking a forest path, listening to what sounded a lot like a couple of guys drowning, and I was having one of those can't-miss days. Tom told me real grouse hunters pushed swamps; I told him smart grouse hunters stayed outside and let the other guy push out the birds. Funny, but I think you had to be there...

There was another time at grouse camp when I accidentally locked Tom's setter, Sadie, in his blazer along with his car keys, then mixed myself a Scotch and watched as Tom tried to ham-handle the door lock with a coat hanger. Sadie waited until he almost had it, then she strolled up to the driver's seat and sort of indifferently ate the steering wheel.

But I think he's still sore about that one. Plus, you

kind of had to be there . . .

It did, though, remind me of the way you just
can't trust dogs, especially hunting dogs. Say what you
want about not turning your back on Rottweilers and
pit bulls and other such warm, fuzzy bundles of canine
dementia. Trust me: No breed is as low-down and
sneaky as a gun dog. Mostly because the bastards
learned it from us. From the time he figured things
were a whole lot easier three-squares-wise on the other
side of the fire, *Canus familiaris* has survived by his
guile and by adapting. Adapting to our ways.

I mean, look at a cow or a pig or a chicken or a
sheep. They don't lie. Or steal from you. Or cheat you
half-blind. What's it get them? Eaten. Real regular.

But your gun dog—your Lab or pointer or Britt or
setter or whatever—will take the food off your table
when you aren't looking, sleep on the good furniture,
particle-ize the evening paper better than the CIA
could do it, dig up your neighbor's tulip bulbs, chase
shrieking school kids to and from the bus stop, and
barf up squirrel parts on your daughter's First
Communion dress. When the minister comes to pay a
visit, Rover spends the afternoon trying to hump his
leg. What's it get him? He gets to live inside, or in a
cozy kennel. He gets his ears scratched and his tummy
rubbed. He gets scraps from the table. We tiptoe over
his snoring form in the middle of the living floor so we

won't wake him; it doesn't matter that his nasal gymnastics sound like a mortar barrage. And we call him things like "Sport" and "Pal" and "King" and "Prince." We've been had, I tell you.

Take for example the Arrested Development, Maggie, a black Lab, that lives at my house. Setters can be haughty and regal and Brittanies friendly and solicitous; pointers are hunting machines, aloof and detached except when the gun and boots come out. But Labs are people. The kind of people your mother didn't want you to play with when you were a kid.

When Maggie was six months old, my two sons had her out pheasant hunting. Cruising a back-country road, they spotted a bunch of roosters in a ditch row and quickly asked for permission to hunt. The farmer told them okay, but noticed the dog and told the guys that they looked like they could tell the difference between a Holstein and a pheasant, but that black dog didn't, and they needed to leave her in the car or no hunting.

Well, what they should have said is that, to them, more than half of their hunting pleasure was hunting with their dog, and if they couldn't, well, thanks just the same. But they're young and eager. So they leave the dog in the car, bail out at the ditch row, load up, and roosters start buzzing out. They're shooting and hollering and loading and laughing. They shoot two or three birds and head back to the car.

Maggie ate the dashboard. All of it. Everything except the oil pressure gauge and the volume knob on the radio.

She pulled the handles off the window winders, and a portion of the upholstery above the passenger's side hung from the roof, and a Garth Brooks tape was a shredded, backlashed memory on the floor.

What a wonderful beast.

The guys came home all aglow about their great shoot and how Mags was going to be a superior dog because her intensity level was so high . . .

Or the time we're duck hunting on an island in Lake Michigan near home, just a long, narrow atoll with some brush and big rocks about a half mile off shore. It's November and the bluebills are buzzing the island. It's also northern Michigan, so there's a stout wind working, though the sky is clear. Pitch dark, about five a.m., and my sons and I are in an over-loaded freight canoe – couple dozen decoys, three guys, three guns, thermoses, shell bags, and You-know-who.

We make it through the waves, which are a few feet high, and pull close to the island into about two feet of water. Naturally, we all stand at once, and the guys get out and start hauling the canoe toward shore. Mags stands on the gunwale, so I shift weight to balance – those of you with fat Labs that can't sit still in a canoe know the drill. As I'm leaning left – toward deep water – the mutt leaps over the side to the right. Between my boots, I get this really breathtaking view of the constellation Orion. I go completely under as the dog paddles happily to shore. The birds are working, so I can't get anyone to help me paddle back. I am forced to invoke the College Tuition Clause and force my own offspring to donate one item of clothing each.

As I strip down to change in the pre-dawn, shivering in the gale, the guys put out the decoys. Maggie brings me a stick and wants to play fetch. As I said, they learned their ways from us. It was like she was rubbing it in.

Which reminds me of the time on a grouse hunt that not only did I manage to get on the dry end of the line, Tom and his brother Chuck were down in the swamp . . .

The Old Ones Are the Best Ones

Galen Winter

Five hunters were sitting around a pot-bellied stove that was only a bit older than any one of them. It was the Thursday night before the Saturday morning opening of the deer season. There was some scotch, bourbon, sour mash, brandy, and dry sherry present.

If it had been Friday evening, the presence of those libations would not have been discernible because the camp rule dictated no drinking on the evening before the opening of the season. But it was Thursday, so an occasional nibble at the jug was acceptable behavior.

Now I don't mean to suggest any of the five were anything close to what even a WCTUer would call a boozer. They were all quite temperate. The fact that five different kinds of beverage have been identified means only that the five did not agree on many things, and each had firm beliefs concerning the relative merits of attitude-adjusting liquids.

The five had hunted together for 25 years, and if

you excluded the youngster (62 years old), the other four had shared that November camp for over 35 years. And just because they didn't always agree did not mean this was an unhappy deer camp. Oh, no. It was a very happy camp. It was a delight to be there.

Though the phrase "You're filled with fecal material" (or something like that) commonly rang out during the post-dinner conversations, the bonds of friendship were never broken. They weren't even strained. Packer and Bear fans coexisted and discussed the relative merits of the two teams in peace (except for a more-than-occasional "You're filled with fecal material").

These old-timers had a secret: They liked each other. It is the younger hunters who more often get their noses out of shape and screw up a deer camp. Don't get me wrong—I'm not against younger hunters. All hunters are good people, but some are better than others, and I believe the old ones are the best ones. They tend to be a bit mellower. For one thing, they've been in a lot of hunting camps and, during the many years of wandering about in the out-of-doors, they've witnessed more than one strange happening. Their longer exposure to life has given them a wide variety of experiences, and it's fun to sit back and listen to them.

Emery had just finished telling how he acquired the bear skin that had hung on the cabin wall since

1964. He told the story once during every one of the subsequent deer seasons. It was an old story, but Emery enjoyed telling it, and we all enjoyed listening to it. The old ones are the best ones.

There was a pause in the conversation.

"Too bad about that hunter down at Gresham last year."

"Was there some trouble?"

"I don't believe I heard about it." "What happened?" "You must have seen it. It was in all of the papers." "Not all of us get the Shawano Evening Leader, Floyd. What happened?" Well, this diplomat - I believe he was a member of the Czechoslovakian Consulate in Chicago - was a consummate deer hunter. According to the story, he had hunted with a group out of Gresham for five or six years and knew his way around the woods.

"Apparently he and his campmates formed a very close-knit group. It was like this camp. Everyone looked out for everyone else.

"Remember the cold snap at the end of last year's season? It must have gotten down to ten below. No civilized person would hunt in such teeth-shattering conditions. The diplomat suited up and walked out towards his stand. Like I say, he was a consummate deer hunter.

"During the evening meal, at about seven o'clock

when the meat was all gone, someone noticed an empty chair at the table. After discussion, it was decided the consular official was the one who was missing. By ten o'clock, some of his campmates thought he may have been lost.

"They drove a few of the roads around their hunting territory and blew the horn, but heard no response - possibly because the windows in the car were rolled up in order to keep the occupants toasty warm. (It was still a bit below zero outside — a temperature they considered to be far too cold for a foot-search of the area.) "The following morning the thermometer had climbed to a more pleasant 35 degrees, and after a leisurely noon luncheon (and a vote of five in favor and four against) a search team was organized. When the hunters arrived at the diplomats usual stand, a scene of bloody gore assaulted their eyes.

"They found a rifle with a broken stock, bits of flesh and blood-soaked clothing, one tooth-marked and lacerated boot, and the foot prints of two bear. The disturbed red snow gave evidence of the terrible fight that must have occurred. Of course, the hunters tracked down the two animals and dispatched them.

"Feeling they should give the Czech's remains a

decent burial, his campmates opened the sow and searched her stomach contents. No trace of the diplomat was found. Then they turned their attentions to the other beast and, sure enough, the Czech was in the male."

(Editor's Note: The old ones are the best ones.)

The Muskox and the Man
from Long Island

John Barsness

Contrary to what many believe, male muskoxen can be very dangerous, particularly during the August-September rut. Every year, one or two people are tromped and horned by angry bulls. This was made quite plain to us by our Inuit guides the late August evening we flew into the camp on the Ellice River in the Northwest Territories, but evidently it didn't get through to the hunter from Long Island. He was the one who complained about the food on the airplane, told the camp taxidermist he knew more about taxidermy than anyone alive, and bitched like Zsa Zsa when he found out the camp didn't have a shower. (Showers are very rare in primitive hunting camps 200 miles north of the Arctic Circle.) Early the next morning, before the guides arrived, a muskox bull wandered between the guest cabins. The man from Long Island grabbed his telephoto-equipped camera and went after it, despite warnings from the rest of us. I watched through my spotting scope as he chased the bull. The muskox was walking steadily away across the tundra, but our Long Islander wanted a frontal shot, so he shouted and ran toward the critter. By now the cameraman and his subject were 600 yards from camp, too far for anyone to shoot the muskox if it charged. The bull turned and looked, then put its head down and waggled its horns. The man from long Island aimed his camera. The muskox pawed the earth. The man from Long Island clicked off a few more. The muskox advanced, using all the standard body language of angry bovids everywhere, snorting and pawing and hooking its horns, and still the man from Long Island clicked on. Then he sat down, evidently to steady the camera. The muskox picked its head up with an astonished look, and then turned and ran off.

In the meantime, the head guide had shown up and was watching, wide-eyed, sure he'd have to call in an emergency flight to haul out another busted-up muskox hunter. The guide quietly lectured the man from Long Island when he returned, who dismissed the guide, saying, "These muskoxes ain't ever met anyone from New York. They wouldn't survive two minutes in Manhattan!" Maybe he had a point. By the end of the week the man from Long Island complained about the food so much that the cook had threatened to take off certain of his parts with an ulu, the Inuit skinning knife, and one of the other hunters had threatened to toss him in the Arctic Ocean. But the man from Long Island got on the flight back to Kennedy Airport with all his body parts, and a muskox, still bitching about the food, the help, the weather, and every other thing he could imagine.

But I don't think he should go back. The cook was last seen sharpening her ulu. He wouldn't last two minutes up there.

Hunting the Naugahyde

Craig Boddington

My first experience with the strange beast they call the blue bull—properly a nilgai, less properly a "Naugahyde," as Tom Siatos dubbed them—came during a Remington writers' seminar in south Texas some years ago.

Remington gave us options. We could hunt white-tail deer or select only one animal from a list of several exotic species. One of the animals on the list was the nilgai. No one knew much about the species, even though nilgai are entirely free-ranging in Texas. They are confined almost exclusively to the Coastal Plains—ranches that were part of or neighbor to the great King Ranch when nilgai were first introduced in 1932. Few outsiders hunt that country even to this day, and a decade ago none of this group of America's foremost writers had ever shot a nilgai.

Since it was something different, even though no one knew what they were, fully a half dozen writers chose to hunt nilgai. The featured rifle that year was a

Remington Model 700 Mountain Rifle. And since the hottest new load Remington had that year was the 140-grain Pointed Soft Point for the .280, we were all issued rifles in that caliber and ammunition in that bullet weight.

What ensued was the biggest wreck I have seen in my hunting career, before or since. Nilgai are almost elk-sized, and more than elk-tough. Worse, like sable and roan antelope, they are all shoulder, sloping sharply down to fairly narrow hips. By day's end, all over the ranch there were mildly pissed nilgai nursing minor wounds from the .280 fly swatters. Only one writer did indeed drop his bull—with a neck shot. Another got his, but he was fortunate to catch a bull in an opening that allowed him to empty his rifle into it. The rest of the bulls were still running. Even the neck shot bull is suspect, for this was a youngster taken for the superb meat. Mature nilgai bulls are immensely bigger than cows and immature females.

On another occasion while hunting whitetails in that country, I was lying on a levee, drooling over a fine whitetail bedded on the far side of a stock tank, just too far to shoot and totally unapproachable. To the buck's left was a herd of nilgai, also resting in the shade. Most of those visible were brown cows and fawn-colored youngsters, but there were a few almost-blue young bulls and a couple of almost-black mature bulls. Then, while we watched, Grandfather stood from his bed. He towered over his cows and the other bulls. It was like Godzilla rising from his lair, and that bull nilgai was perhaps the most imposing creature I have ever seen. There is simply no comparison between an old fully mature bull and the rest of the species.

The day after the wreck, I recovered one of the wounded nilgai. We spotted him by a water hole, and I crept up behind him and spined him with the little .280. It is well that I did. He had taken a perfectly centered shoulder shot—but the shoulder ate the bullet, and the inside of the rib cage wasn't even bruised.

I became fascinated by nilgai and hunted them several times over the next few years. I even introduced John Wootters to them, taking great pleasure in showing a dyed-in-the-brush-country Texan a new game animal in his own state. Wootters and I discovered that nilgai aren't bulletproof. The first time we hunted them, his bull succumbed – not readily, but finally – to a .340 Weatherby. Mine succumbed much the same to a .338. The next time we hunted them we each used a .416, finally finding enough gun. Bob Petersen, Tom Siatos, and Ken Elliott also hunted them, but each used a .375; they came away thinking my tales of nilgai toughness were all exaggeration. That's what the old saying "use enough gun" really means!

To Hell With the Queen

John Barsness

When I was much younger, an older man and I made annual fishing trips to Saskatchewan, camping in a wall tent on the edge of a long lake and trolling after walleyes and northern pike. One year we'd just arrived and stopped in the local post office cum hardware-grocery-sporting-goods store to buy a few lures, beans and licenses. It was a typical small town Canadian store with customers from 20 miles around picking up mail and buying a few supplies, under a tinted black-and-white photograph of Queen Elizabeth.

After we piled everything on the counter, the owner of the store rang our purchases up on the cash register, then–by way of explaining the sales tax–said, "And that'll be fifty cents extra for the Queen." Without a second's hesitation, my partner said, rather loudly, "To hell with the Queen." The whole store stopped. Everybody turned our way, and the store owner stared in silence for a long moment, then cleared his throat and said, "Mister, I've been wanting to say that myself for a long, long time."

The Secret Trout Place
(The Trade)

Bill Vaznis

Have you ever noticed that strangers expect sports writers to know everything about hunting and fishing? People often come right up to me and ask me how I catch so many trout in the summertime. I don't want to steer them wrong, so I tell them they have to work hard at it. I mean, I tell them to study topo maps to see where 4X4 trails cross small streams, and then walk upstream, or I tell them to walk along the banks of major streams and look for shaded areas and underground springs.

But if you want to know the truth, the best way to find a honey hole is to ask someone who knows, like my friend Bob LaPalme. He fishes all the headwaters, beaver dams, and spring-fed creeks in the county, and has for years. If the trout are congregated anywhere in the summertime, he knows where they are. The only trouble is getting him to tell you. I've tried everything over the years, including getting him drunk, all to no avail. Last summer, though, I hit upon his weakness. You see, Bob also likes to hunt woodcock, so I offered (okay, bribed) to trade him a day at an old abandoned farm soon after the first good cold snap up north for a day of trout fishing in one of his July honey holes. After a few hours of arm twisting, Bob finally took the bait. He agreed to go fishing with me right after the next heavy thundershower.

I picked him up just after breakfast the next day, and then headed out to parts unknown. He didn't seem to notice the roads were dry. Anyway, we seemed to be driving in circles for over an hour before Bob eventually recognized the turn-off.

I jacked on the brakes, backed up, and then parked the 4X4 along the shoulder of the old logging road. I fumbled with the ignition, finally shutting it off, and then started to get out when Bob grabbed me by the shoulder. "Now listen to me, you crazy Lithuanian," he said. "Not a word about this spot to anybody, understand? No articles!"

"I promise I won't tell a soul," I replied with a smile. "After all, if it's as good as you say it is, I want to keep it a secret, too. Okay buddy?" Bob just stared at me. I knew what he was thinking about just by the look on his face: Would I jeopardize our forty years of friendship for one trout hot spot? We proceeded to unload our gear, making sure we had enough insect repellent and small spinners to last the morning. Then, after donning rain coats end light-weight rubber boots, we crossed the dirt road and headed off into the woods.

Since there was no path, I dutifully followed Bob's lead—but not without periodically checking my backtrail with a compass. You see, I knew Bob was going to protect his private fishing grounds from any future intrusions by taking the long way to the stream. First he zigzagged to the east, and then he turned left by a big sugar maple and walked due north for ten minutes or so, only to go east again. (I wrote all this down.) Finally, after muttering unconvincingly, "I think it's over here somewhere," he "stumbled" upon an overgrown trail that eventually took us to within earshot of the creek. When we heard the roar of the current, my step quickened with anticipation (okay, I ran), until I finally stood on the bank of Can't-Tell-You Brook.

Once there, it was my turn to stare, for Bob's often-talked-about honey hole was an incredibly beautiful stretch of deep runs and whitewater riffles. Upstream, water sped swiftly through a narrow gorge where it cascaded over moss-covered rocks and huge granite boulders—some half as big as a truck—before tumbling freely past us into a series of deep bubbly pools that stretched downstream as far as the eye could see. And these pools, as I found out, were teeming with hungry, dark-backed brook trout the likes of which I hadn't seen since I was a kid.

We cast small spinners till dark, hooking and releasing dozens of fat wild trout, and then, after quenching our thirst with some homemade lemonade Bob had stored in his cellar all winter, we headed back to the truck. Me, I had a big smile on my face, for this spot was really a great fishing hole. But Bob, who led our way down the path with a flashlight, seemed to be lost in thought. Surprisingly, it only took us a few minutes to get back to civilization.

"Too bad we couldn't fish the other fork," said Bob, suddenly feeling guilty about showing me one of his honey holes. "There are some deeper pools there and a couple of whitewater riffles that make the fishing there really hot this time of year. It's probably the best spot in the county for native brookies. In fact, I've caught two that came close to four pounds there so far. Margie and I are going on vacation next week, and then my cousin is getting married.

"Maybe we can fish it this fall after you take me woodcock hunting. Where did you say you flushed all those birds last year?"

"I didn't say," I replied, "but I don't think it's too far from here. Let's come back this fall and fish that other fork you talked about until noon, and then grab the dogs and hunt the old farm I bragged, I mean talked to you about till dark."

From the look on his face, Bob had taken the bait again, but this time I only had him hooked in the lip. I knew right then and there I had to call Pete Kunda when I got home. He loves to hunt birds, and knows all the best cover in the county. He once told me over shots and a couple dozen beers about an abandoned farm he's been to where the woodcock are thick soon after a cold snap up north. Of course, in exchange for that information, I'd be sure to ask Pete if he would like to go trout fishing with me at my secret honey hole some time this summer.

The Heebie-Jeebies

Jerry Dennis

I remember laying awake one night in 1975 in a small tent in the Yellowstone back country. Mike McCumby and I had hiked there in the morning and spent the day climbing after bighorn sheep on a mountainside, examining the scat of elk and coyote and bear, finally setting up camp beside a pond full of grayling and rainbow trout.

Mike slept the good sleep of the innocent while I, excited by the day's explorations, lay warm and comfortable in my sleeping bag, listening to the breeze in the lodgepole pines and thinking about things. After a while I stopped thinking about things and started thinking about grizzly bears, which is a natural thing to do in a tent in the remote corners of Yellowstone. Those corners are, of course, grizzly country, a fact that until then had bothered me very little.

The history of back country camping in Yellowstone is a long and bright one, and I knew there was very little chance of encountering a bear. But knowing it and believing it are very different things, and the more I thought it over, the jumpier I became. Mike's easy, instant sleep had been amusing at first; now it seemed a betrayal. If he was any kind of friend, I reasoned, he would be awake to keep me company.

Then I heard a noise.

I have spent enough nights alone in a tent to know how imagination can amplify ordinary pounds. If you are sufficiently spooked, a pair of raccoons fumbling with a cooler latch can sound like a Wyoming bar fight. Still, this seemed a significant noise, a notable noise. I considered it as objectively as possible. It was not a loud sound, not a definitive sound, just something out of audible place. On consideration, it seemed precisely the kind of furtive noise a very large creature would make if it did not want to be heard.

Now there came a large noise. Not a loud noise, a large noise, the sound of something very large stepping quietly on padded feet. Then definitely (Oh! definitely) the sound of air being inhaled through spacious nostrils.

Dryness clenched my throat. It was impossible to swallow. Inside my chest, my heart galloped like a rodent trapped in an empty five-gallon bucket. Every cell of my body stood erect, listening. My eyes strained in vain to see something, anything, in the blackness inside the tent. I waited for a single exquisite claw to rent the fabric and open the wall of the tent, like a surgeon's scalpel slicing the cellophane that encloses a Hostess cupcake. I visualized the event so clearly, I was unsure whether it had yet happened.

Two shambling revolutions around the tent and now a snuffling noise, as of sinus trouble.

Because I knew Mike would not want to die in the terrible oblivion of sleep, I tried to wake him. I whispered his name. The sound came out with so little volume it was not really a sound at all. Mike might have thought, were he awake, that he had heard a field mouse yawning. He might have thought he heard the whispery voice of an ancestor buried six generations in his family's past. I tried again. The sound produced was less vocalization than telepathy, the message originating in my solar plexus but not pushed out by breath. I had no breath. My lungs hung void of air, like becalmed sails, the space inside my chest occupied only by the frantic leaping chaos of that trapped rodent.

Slowly, cautiously, I raised my arm from inside my sleeping bag and reached for Mike. I punched him. I punched him again, harder.

"What? What is it?" he said, his voice terribly, unbearably loud.

"Quiet. Bear. I think. Outside." Mike probed in the darkness for his backpack, found a flashlight, and climbed from his sleeping bag. He unzipped the tent and poked his head out. He switched on the light. There was a pause, a very long pause. He came back inside and zipped the tent closed again.

"Porcupine," he said.

There was nothing, of course, I could say. I tried to chuckle, but failed. For a moment I wondered if it would have been better had there been a bear. A grizzly. Snarling when Mike blinded it with the flashlight.

Mike settled back into his sleeping bag and switched the light off. The darkness seemed more complete, if that was possible. I thought about the nature of fear, how you can never remember afterwards quite how it was. It's like trying to remember a smell: The gulf between the memory and the reality is too great to cross. Already I was beginning to forget just how frightened I had been.

"Yep, a porcupine," Mike said quietly. "Big one, though."

Charged in Africa

John Barsness

We have all read and heard tales of the toughness of African game and the danger of hunting tough beasts that can kill us. We've also read stories claiming those claims are bull, that African game is no tougher than like-sized American game, and that charges only occur with the rarity of solar eclipses.

It was my first evening in Africa, on a ranch in the northern Transvaal, and after dinner my host asked if my partner and I would like to do "a little night-run." A night-run, it turned out, was a jacklighting expedition for small game: scrub hares (exactly like our jackrabbits) and springhaases (like a jackrabbit-sized cross between a gray squirrel and a kangaroo) that the black ranch workers liked to eat. We said yes, and loaded a .223 into a Land Cruiser.

My turn came first, a shot at a scrub hare standing 50 yards away in the spotlight. I aimed carefully, right behind the shoulder, because we were using bullets designed for small antelope that wouldn't tear up much meat, and squeezed off. The shot looked good, but the hare just stood there, a puff of dust drifting slowly off behind its shoulder.

"Let's get closer, chaps," my host said, driving in a circle behind the hare. Just about the time I was going to shoot again, the bunny fell over, kicking. We got out and picked it up. The bullet had been placed perfectly, and just about all its inner organs were lying on the ground. They are tough! I thought.

Now it was my partner's turn. A half mile farther along a springhaas bounced in front of the headlights, into a brush pile ten feet across. While I wielded the spotlight, he and our host got out and approached the brush. My partner aimed at the springhaas' head and shot, and the animal came straight out of the brush, teeth bloody, right for them. There was no time for a second shot; at the last second our host kicked the wild-eyed beast ten feet into the air. Upon landing, it ran right toward me, standing in the open with nothing but a spotlight in my hands. I readied my boot, but at the last second the springhaas veered into another patch of brush, where my partner shot it again. This time it ran the other way, more slowly, and our host chased it down and stepped on its neck. He took his knife from its sheath and bent down to slit the spring-haas's throat and end this adventure—and the spring-haas bit him, right through the ball of the thumb.

148

So, if anyone tells you African game isn't tough or that charges are incredibly rare, tell him about the toughness of scrub hares and the ferocious five-pound springhaas. Of course, don't tell them about all the other game we killed that week, up to 700 pounds or so, that fell to one shot. And don't ask me my opinion on the subject. All I know is that we were charged our very first night in Africa and were lucky to have escaped with thumbs intact.

The Inuit and the Grizzly

Bill Vaznis

That reminds me of the time I was on the tundra, bowhunting for caribou. I had taken a floatplane an hour and a half or so north of Yellowknife to a small outpost camp on Little Marten Lake. There were plenty of caribou around, and the cold water was chock full of half-starved lake trout. It was nothing to land a few good ones before dinner by cruising the shoreline with a spinning rod and a three-inch Jack of Diamonds.

There were other critters along the shore looking for food, too—grizzlies. Steve Cook, our camp manager, told us one had to be destroyed a few days before our arrival because it had ventured too close to camp. Actually, the big bruin walked right into camp and was shot somewhere near my tent.

That night, our first in camp, was a joyous occasion. There were a dozen hunters from all across the country, and we wiled away the afterdinner hours asking about the caribou migration and where the hunters before us had tagged out. We were also assigned guides. Now, I would rather hunt alone, especially with a bow, but the threat of grizzlies made it mandatory that we not leave camp without a guide and a rifle.

I was teamed up with a young Inuit named Andy, and Bob Lloyd, a well-known taxidermist from Edmonton. Andy had never guided before, but he showed us a map of the region, and after studying the black and brown squiggles for a while, we decided to take a motorboat across the lake in the morning to hunt a series of rocky ridges that paralleled the shore. It looked ideal because there was more than enough cover there for a bowhunter to get close to a meandering caribou. Besides, Andy said he saw a lot of bulls there just before dark.

Unfortunately, by morning all the caribou seemed to be out on the open plains, and we couldn't get to within 200 yards of any of them without being spotted. The caribou were there the next day too, but stalking them was out of the question, even if it was just Andy and I after them. By the end of the third day, I had seen over 5,000 caribou but had not drawn an arrow. Time was running short, and I knew if I was ever going to get a crack at a good bull with my bow, I would have to have Andy stay behind me a hundred yards or so. This was something the young Inuit was not willing to do, however. "Grizzly," was all he would say, and he continued to walk in my shadow.

The next morning, Bob and I popped record book bulls with Bob's 7mm magnum. Bob stayed in camp the rest of the day, caping the heads, while I continued on with my bow. That afternoon, I spotted a white-maned bull a half mile below me, feeding along the shore of one of the many small lakes that dot the tundra. He was stalkable, but still too far away for me to accurately judge his rack.

I asked Andy to stay put while I tried to put the sneak on the bull. If he was a good one, I would signal Andy to come down after I shot. Otherwise, I would return as soon as possible. Andy was not happy. He knew I was getting frustrated with him tagging along so close behind me. Only after I assured him I would not under any circumstances venture out of his sight did he shrug his shoulders and agree with my plan.

When I topped the last small ridge that hid the bull, I was surprised to see that he was gone. I glassed the nearby terrain to no avail. Then I swung my Zeiss binoculars along the top of an esker that bordered the far side of the lake, just in time to see a chocolate-brown grizzly come over the top in my direction. To say he was huge would be an understatement. He looked like Jaws in a fur coat, and I was suddenly very happy the lake separated us by a few hundred yards.

I looked back up the hill for Andy, but I couldn't see him anywhere. Helluva time to have to take a dump, I thought, and I turned my attention back to the grizzly. The bear stood on top of the esker for a few more minutes as if he were surveying his kingdom, and then laid down with his huge head between his paws. He looked peaceful, and it seemed obvious he was going to be there for a while.

Suddenly Andy appeared behind me with his rifle at the ready. "Grizzly," I whispered, and pointed over at the esker.

Andy's voice was filled with anxiety. "I know," he answered. "I saw him sneaking along the other side of the esker and came down to help you."

"What's he doing?" I asked.

"Let's go right now," he said. "The bear is hungry and he is looking for camp."

"Wait a minute," I said. "What about sneaking around the lake and trying to get a picture of that bear? We could get the wind in our favor, cross that brush-choked draw and maybe get close enough for a few photographs with my telephoto lens." Andy looked at me like I'd been eating too many raw fish eggs. I could see the idea terrified him.

A few minutes later, Andy and I were trying to circle around the bear. After we had halved the distance, I looked back to get my bearings, only to find the bear gone. We frantically began looking around for him when suddenly we spotted that grizzly running full tilt right at us. Now we were both terrified.

It's strange what the brain does at moments like this. All I could think of was the remark I once made to a friend back home. I had told him I would rather be mauled by a grizzly than be crushed in a car accident. What a stupid thing to say, I thought. It would be much better to die while sleeping–comfortably sleeping–in my own bed. I really had no desire to become bowhunter burger.

The thought of imminent pain snapped me back to reality. There was no place to hide, and I certainly couldn't outrun the bear, not with 60 pounds of camera gear in my pack.

That's when Andy opened the bolt part way on his scoped rifle. I hadn't thought much about his gun until that point. I could see he had a shell in the chamber and a few more in the magazine. "What caliber?" I asked.

"Two-twenty-three," was all he replied.

"Is that scope on?"

His eyes the size of dinner plates, he answered, "I've never shot the gun before." Damn! The bear entered the brush-choked draw, and I went into a state of suspended animation as I waited for him to make his exit and continue on with his charge. I watched in slow motion as one yellow-leafed willow after another gave way to his bulk.

And then all was still. A minute went by, and then another passed. Only then did we realize the bear was not after us. He had apparently gotten our wind when he was resting on the esker and was more afraid of us than we were of him. He was, in fact, heading for the draw all along. When he got there, he disappeared from our lives forever.

Andy carried that .223 at port arms for the rest of the day, and every time I turned around to see where Andy was, I found him way behind me, looking back at that brush-choked draw. He didn't want the bear sneaking up on us, he said.

That night back at camp, Bob asked me if I was able to get close to any caribou. No, I told him, but there was still one more day left in the hunt, and there were some caribou back on the other side of the lake. Then he asked me if Andy was still guiding out of my hip pocket. If he is, he said, maybe he could talk with Steve and get me another guide. I'll stick with Andy, I told him. He sees more caribou than I do, and he certainly has my best interests at heart. Besides, I think I found a way to keep him at bay. All I have to do is look behind me every once in a while and ask him what that fuzzy brown thing is behind the rock.

Bob and I had a good laugh over that, but before we turned in, I asked him if Andy could borrow his 7mm in the morning.

Confession of the
Woodchuck Stalker

Robert Elman

For almost as long as I can remember, I've had an intense fondness for woodchucks. I like just watching them in a pasture, the way they punctuate their preoccupied gluttony with sudden pauses to sit upright and look about for danger. I like eating them. I've been told they don't compare with rabbit, and that's true. Chuck is better, and there's more of it. Most of all, I like hunting them. But 1 have to confess I'll never be one of those superlative long-range riflemen to whom the "x" in *Marmota monax* stands for X-ring. Although I've skewered a chuck or two at 300 yards, my idea of fun is to stalk close enough to pot one with a rimfire handgun or even an arrow. I dispatched my first groundhog when I was 10 years old and, so help me, I did it with a Red Ryder BB gun.

My wife nags me to prove it by using my son's Daisy to get rid of the chuck that keeps digging under our barn, but I don't have the heart. She's been with us for three years, she's almost like one of the family, and her offspring don't hang around for more than a season, so the pasture doesn't suffer much. Besides, I hold that it takes a boy to do a boy's work. As far as I'm concerned, the fate of our barn tenant is in my son's hands.

About that chuck I killed when I was 10–you'll say it must have been sick or injured if it didn't scurry down its burrow in time to escape, but I prefer to think I was the Daniel Boone of my pre-pubescent world. After all, a year later I stalked gray squirrels and knocked them out of beech trees with a .22 Benjamin air rifle. I believe there's a magic power in boyhood that dissipates with age. There was, however, a day in the 1970s when a chuck convinced me I'd recaptured both boyhood and Boonehood.

At that time my wife and I had a cabin in the Poconos where we hunted and fished. Ellen, being a professional musician, also played concerts in the area with a chamber-music quintet. Performances were held periodically at an estate whose owner supported the arts by allowing a building to be used as a concert hall. My attendance was more or less optional, but I enjoyed the music as a change of pace from Hank Williams, Loretta Lynn, and the real classics, Lester Flatt and Earl Scruggs, so I drove over in my pickup one afternoon for a matinee performance. I was alone,

Ellen having gone on ahead to rehearse.

A dirt road snaked through the estate, past the caretaker's cottage, and as I came around a bend I noticed a big, lubberly chuck chomping clover about 60 yards from the cottage. I had no gun or bow in the rack, but with half an hour to kill before the concert I decided to see how close I could stalk. I drove past the next bend and headed back on foot. My only cover consisted of a few low shrubs, but I took full advantage of them as I circled to put the breeze in my face.

I moved very slowly, crouching, then crawling, taking care not to snap a twig or roll a pebble. The chuck was chin-deep in clover, munching away in a hypnotic trance of gluttony, never rising up on its haunches, moving very little and always in one direction, into the breeze. The animal had been inching away from safety as it mowed the grass. It had wandered at least 10 yards from the bald delta of its main burrow entrance, but seemed to sense no danger whatever.

The stalk took me almost 20 minutes, and as I came closer I felt an excitement as intense as if I were stalking big game. I yearned to count coup by touching that chuck. Yes, touching it! Why not? Nothing is impossible for a resurrected Boy Boone. Surely if anyone could do it, I could! And I very nearly did. My left hand, trembling now, was inches from its rotund back when it finally realized something was up and waddled, then lunged for its hole.

I laughed and stood up. Damn if I wasn't pleased with myself. If I hadn't quite touched it, I had come within inches. Then, as I turned to leave, I saw I had an audience. Two round-cheeked and portly ladies, rather marmotlike themselves, had stopped their car on their way to the concert. No doubt they had noticed me crawling as they came around the last bend and had stopped to watch my strange behavior. They must have witnessed all or most of my performance, but I'd been too preoccupied to see or hear their car. They waved coquettishly and then drove on. I walked back to the pickup and proceeded to the concert.

At intermission, a covey of fluttering matrons suddenly surrounded me. One of them asked for my autograph! Evidently the ladies who had watched me in the caretaker's pasture had made inquiries and discovered I was the soloist's husband. In answer to their questions, Ellen had told them I was an "outdoor writer and amateur naturalist." They weren't merely impressed; they were awed. Those two women who had stopped, watching from a distance, thought I really had touched that chuck—petted it, in fact.

For a very brief moment I considered correcting them, but I've always felt it's cruel to disillusion people. I mean, we all need heroes to prove the unat-

tainable can be attained, don't we? I was their hero, a
gentle woodland sorcerer with the wisdom and power
to approach, touch, communicate with wild creatures.

Just as the bell tinkled to signal the end of intermission, a graying, wind-wrinkled man in a green work
shirt and chino pants squirmed past my admirers,
excusing himself politely as he extended his hand.
Introducing himself as the caretaker, he remarked that
he had heard about my encounter with the wood-
chuck.

"How close did you get?" he asked.

"Oh, close enough to touch him," I said, grinning
with the pride of achievement and celebrity. Then,
with unnecessary modesty, I added, "You'd have
thought he was blind, deaf, and had no sense of smell."

"Well," the man said, "I wouldn't know about his
sense of smell, but I can see you're an observant naturalist, all right. Got no idea how old he is—been in that
pasture for years. Used to think he was a her, 'cause he
never wandered off looking for a mate. He's back in
that pasture every spring and summer. But there's
never been any youngsters. Could be a barren female,
but I guess it's a male, all right."

"You sure it's the same one year after year?" I
asked.

"No doubt about it. Can't figure out how he man-
ages to avoid the hawks and foxes. We never realized

he was deaf till last summer, when we got Tinkerbell and she set up a racket barking at him. He didn't pay her the slightest mind. Always been pretty tame, but not like he's been lately. Lets my wife walk right up and stroke him. Did you get a look at his eyes? He's blind, all right. Probably won't last another summer, and that's one pet we'll hate to lose. Angus, we call him—not that he answers to it. If you'd like to pet him, come on over for coffee after the concert."

An Arctic Adventure

Jim Zumbo

"**W**here the hell are we?" one of my companions asked as our Inuit guide eased the freighter canoe slowly amidst the jagged rocks. It was practically pitch black; we were floating an uncharted shoreline of the Arctic ocean, and we were damned concerned.

At least Vin and I were. Salamonie Jaw, our Inuit guide, told us in broken English that there was nothing to fear, that he'd find camp in short order.

A few moments later, the canoe slammed into a rock. It wasn't a wrenching blow that knocked us off our feet, but more of an abrupt thud that put us at instant alert. A quick check with a flashlight revealed no damage to the canoe, but the incident didn't exactly add to our confidence level in terms of locating camp.

Salamonie continued piloting the canoe, guided by an intuitive Eskimo instinct that allowed him to navigate through the rocks. He was doing a perfect job. Almost.

A tense hour passed when Salamonie pointed off

in the distance.

"Camp," he said.

The word came out as though he was asking someone to pass the ketchup.

Vin and I were not in such a tranquil mood. The discovery of our camp area was a whole lot more exciting to us.

"Where!" we both asked in unison.

Salamonie calmly pointed; we saw his arm extended in the faint starlight and looked. Sure enough, something was indeed out there in the dark. A couple small yellow dots suggested lantern lights, but it was so far away, and there were so many rocks in the underwater reefs around us, that we were still in for a mini- adventure before we climbed out of the canoe.

"Camp not far," salamonie said, as if he'd read my mind. "Dark make things look far."

Good news. Salamonie was right, of course. I'd appreciated that phenomenon most of my adult life, but you need to constantly remind yourself that things really aren't as distant as they look at night.

Our canoe nudged against a few more rocks, and finally we were in open water, headed for camp. I was amazed, because Salamonie had never been to that area in his life. Yet, he unerringly charted a course through the reefs and found camp. It was a superb demonstration of the Inuit's sense of direction.

This trip, so far, had all the makings of a major nightmare, and Vin and I wondered aloud many times if we'd ever get the hell out of there in one piece.

We were on Baffin Island, hunting Central Barren Ground caribou. According to Jerome Knap, our outfitter, our party was the first group of American hunters ever to hunt on Baffin island, a fact that explained some of the problems we encountered.

Our group sat in on an orientation meeting in Montreal prior to the trip. During that meeting, Vin Sparano, *Outdoor Life's* editor, and I met Madleine Kay, a California jeweler who specializes in creating wildlife pieces.

Since Madleine didn't know anyone in the party, but she and I knew some mutual friends, she asked if she could share a tent with Vin and me. These were fairly large tents of the type used in the Arctic, and Madleine wasn't terribly interested in living in one solo.

At this point I must add that Madleine's pulchritudinal assets are downright phenomenal: The lady could easily be a centerfold in *Playboy.* Of course, Vin and I were pleased to accommodate her request, and so it was that we became an inseparable trio for the rest of the journey.

The hunt began at Cape Dorset, a small Inuit community on Baffin Island. As soon as we flew in, we

167

immediately went to the shore, where we'd be assigned an Inuit guide. Jerome chose Salamonie as our guide because he was the only one who spoke some English. Being writers, Vin and I hoped to be teamed up with an Inuit with whom we could communicate.

Our canoe was powered by a 35-hp outboard. Its generous 24-foot length and six-foot beam comfortably held the four of us, including our gear. Salamonie seemed to be an affable young man with an easy smile and a fair hand at speaking English. Most importantly, he seemed competent enough to get us to our destination, which was 80 miles away, all of it across the Arctic Ocean.

An elderly Inuit who was designated as chief took the lead. His canoe was trailed by six others, each carrying hunters and gear. We totaled seven Inuits and 18 hunters in all.

As we left the rocky coast, I assumed we'd all be traveling in a party, so that each canoe would be visible. After all, that only made good sense, because several of the Inuit guides had never been to the area we were going to, including Salamonie. Good sense, however, isn't exactly a quality that's seen much in the far North. This isn't a negative critique of the Eskimo people, but a look at reality. As we soon learned, they are so incredibly rugged and self-reliant that they don't use logic in the manner we do.

We'd gone about 10 miles, each canoe a small spot on the ocean, some in front of us and some behind. As we traveled, the canoes became farther and farther apart. Salamonie made no attempt to close the gap; he was perfectly content to do his own thing. The journey itself seemed to be questionable as far as time was concerned. When we asked how long it would take at the outset of the trip, the Inuits threw their hands in the air. It appeared that the weather would dictate our travel time, which, of course, is always a factor on any hunting trip requiring a lengthy journey.

At some point that afternoon, Salamonie decided it was time to take a tea break. In the north, tea replaces coffee and is the traditional drink.

When the guide pointed the canoe toward a rocky bay and left the parade of other canoes, I thought perhaps he wanted to gas up or take a nature break. But when Salamonie beached the canoe and calmly set up a pot on a small propane burner on the canoe floor, I was concerned.

"What are we doing, Salamonie?" I asked pleasantly.

"We drink tea," he responded. "Time for tea." Noting that all the canoes were now well ahead of us, I asked the obvious question.

"Do you know where we're going?" I queried.

"No," he responded simply, and that was that.

Now I was carefully weighing my words, because it was necessary that the Inuit comprehend the next point.

"If you don't know where we're going," I said, "shouldn't we be following the other canoes?"

Salamonie digested that bit of information, and then it appeared that a light went off in his head.

"You right," he said. "No time for tea."

At that our guide put away the tea makings, fired up the outboard, and we were once again cruising along the ocean, but this time the other canoes were barely visible. They were just tiny dots in the huge expanse of sea that was now beginning to come alive. A stiff breeze came up, creating whitecaps and significant rollers. Suddenly the 24-foot craft didn't seem so big anymore as we pitched and lurched in the growing waves.

Shortly afterward, we passed an island that was nothing but a pile of rocks. Amazingly, a bunch of dogs appeared and ran along the shoreline, barking incessantly. This was a sight worth pondering: what were a dozen dogs doing on a small, barren island?

Vin touched Salamonie on the shoulder and pointed to the dogs. The guide seemed to know what the question was going to be.

"Dogs free on island," he said, "not free in town. Always tied up."

"What do they eat?" Madleine asked.

Salamonie shrugged. "Anything," he said. "Every few days somebody brings fish or bones or garbage. Dogs eat good."

Now the rollers grew stronger. The wind picked up considerably, and I began to wonder how much punishment the canoe would take as it rose and fell with the demands of the sea.

Soon Salamonie turned the craft away from the open ocean and headed toward a rocky island. The rest of our party had already pulled up to shore and were breaking out gear as we arrived.

"Sea too strong," Salamonie said. "We stay here until it get quiet." That was perfectly fine with us.

It didn't take long to set up the tent. As added insurance, we tied large rocks all the way around in preparation for the storm that we were expecting. The Inuits are big on radio communications; there was a constant chatter between our camp and other groups scattered in the northland. A serious blow was forecasted.

The wind increased during the night to the point where wondered if our tent would stay erect. Vin, Madleine, and I were quite comfortable, tucked in warm sleeping bags and with a kerosene heater to warm the shelter.

Sometime during the night I felt a serious breeze

171

on my face. A gap had opened in the tent wall, allowing the cold air in. The wind was now almost gale
force, tearing at the ropes and fabric with mighty gusts.
Vin and I worked to repair the tent wall, and I can
recall the eerie feeling as I toiled outside. Illuminated
in the starlight were the rest of the tents, each of them
protecting humans inside. The ocean raged a few yards
away, and the wind seethed through our remote outpost. It amazed me that we were where we were,
toughing out a storm that would have killed us if we
didn't have proper shelters. Indeed, the Inuits were
survivors.

That point was driven home more clearly the
next day when our entire group of guides left camp in
two boats, leaving the rest of us to wonder what in hell
was going on. The wind had subsided some, but not
enough to risk taking on the rest of the journey, especially a 25-mile crossing that would move us through
an enormous open-water area with no islands to run to
in case of danger. The crossing would have to be made
in reasonably calm water.

We heard distant shots a couple hours after the
guides had left, but we had no clue what they were up
to. They finally showed up several hours later, the
bows of their canoes splatting the heaving ocean swells
as they made their way back to our island.

Salamonie nonchalantly told us what they'd done.

"We shoot geese and ducks," he said, "and cook them in pot. Good stuff."

After further inquiry, the Inuit told us that he and his pals had killed some waterfowl, tossed them in a pot of boiling water, feathers and innards and all, and ate them after they had cooked a bit.

The fact that the Inuits left all their puzzled hunters in camp without any explanation of their plans made no difference. For all we knew, we were abandoned forever on the island. Interesting people, these Inuits. I was liking them more and more as time passed.

Salamonie pulled a stunt the next day that I still rave about to friends. Underway to our hunting camp once again, he'd spotted some ducks flying in front of the canoe. He grabbed a very rusted .22 that leaned against the gunwale, and drew a bead on one of the ducks. Mind you, we are in a craft that's crashing down from one wave to the other. The Inuit is using a rifle that looks like it sunk with the Titanic. You can imagine our astonishment when the little .22 bullet hit the duck smartly and sent it plummeting into the ocean. Vin, Madleine, and I looked at each other in amazement. Never in my life had I seen such an incredible shot.

Soon it was time to cross the big bay. Luck was on our side, since the ocean calmed somewhat and the crossing was easily accomplished. Icebergs drifted about, and seals romped around our boat. A couple hunters had seal tags, but none were able to connect. I was disappointed, because I wanted to see how the seals were processed by the Eskimos.

Finally we neared camp. As we pulled up to the shore, a few bull caribou ran off over a little rise. Some of the hunters could stand it no longer, and despite a bit of advice to hold off until we spotted bigger bulls, they'd have none of it. Fifteen minutes later, several shots rang out. The hunt was over for a half dozen hunters who'd scored on mediocre bulls.

Since it was late in the day when we arrived, we set up camp and were in no hurry to hunt. The next morning would come soon enough.

As we cruised away from camp soon after sunup, a lone bull appeared in the tundra close to shore. Salamonie gave the thumbs-up sign, but we weren't too sure. We'd been told that the Inuits had no experience in trophy hunting – to them a small bull or cow or calf was prime meat. They seldom killed older bulls, and since we were the first hunters they'd ever guided, they weren't into evaluating antlers.

Nonetheless, the bull looked fine to us, and Vin made a stalk. His bull was down soon afterward, and we loaded it into the canoe after dressing it.

Salamonie, Madleine, and I made a trek over-

174

land, and Vin tagged along as observer. Suddenly, I saw a tree branch in the bottom of a steep slope, but the thought occurred to me that there were no trees in the tundra. A bull caribou emerged. The branch was an antler. Another bull appeared, and both looked very good.

Figuring our hunt was over, Madleine and I stalked close. I suggested she shoot first and take the bull of her choice, but she declined.

"Not good enough," she said. "I'll bet we can do better."

I was amazed, but I trusted her judgement. As an artist who created caribou images as well as other big game, she was schooled in antler configuration. I wasn't about to challenge her opinion.

We took off in the canoe to try another area, this time splitting up. I went off alone while Vin accompanied Madleine and Salamonie.

I'd just reached the top of a ridge when a caribou jumped up and took off. My instinct was to shoot, simply because a running animal often clouds one's judgement and stimulates the adrenaline. I couldn't resist, and put the animal down.

Fifteen minutes later I heard a shot from Madleine's direction. She'd scored too, but her bull was fantastic. As we learned later, it was the best bull taken among our party.

That evening, with the caribou loaded in the canoe, we were beset with another dilemma. The tide was out, and there was no way to move the canoe to the waterline, even if we emptied it.

Without a load it still weighed close to a half ton.

When the tide finally rose to meet the canoe several hours later, we were on our way, but our journey to camp would be in the dark, which brings us around to the beginning of this story.

That evening, as was the case every evening, a couple Inuit guides would come into our tent. No knocking, no greetings – nothing – they just came in. Then they'd sit for a while and stare at the three of us as we played cards, cleaned rifles, or made small talk. To this day I have no idea what prompted this surveillance; perhaps they'd never seen such a beautiful woman before or perhaps they couldn't figure why she was sharing a tent with two men. Or maybe they believed we'd offer her to them. Whatever the case, it was most amusing. I regret I didn't have a translator around to interpret what they were saying when they came over for their nightly visits.

When it was time to pack up and leave, we made another interesting discovery. Behind the tent the Inuits lived in was a large pile of raw, meatless caribou ribs. Evidently they'd eaten the rib meat as a delicacy. Further proof of the survival skills of the Inuits.

176

Salamonie made a most distressing announcement as we loaded the canoe.

"Maybe not have enough gas to get home," he said with amazing calmness.

"What should we do?" I said, noting that several other canoes, some of which held extra gas, were taking off for the 80-mile journey.

"My brother maybe have more gas," Salamonie said.

I had no idea Salamonie's brother was among our party.

"Where's your brother?" I asked.

Salamonie looked at the remaining Inuits who hadn't left, then gazed out into the ocean.

"Out there," Salamonie responded, pointing to a boat half a mile distant and racing away. We'd never catch up, since we had another half hour's work to do before we could leave.

It occurred to me that Salamonie hadn't done any advance thinking about the issue of inadequate gas, but he had a solution that might work.

"If we make it through cut with tide high, we maybe get home," he said. "If tide low and we have to go around, we don't get home. Run out of gas."

"Then what?" Salamonie had no answer. He simply shrugged.

The cut was actually a 15-yard gap in a 20 mile-long peninsula. Making it through the cut should have been a top priority, but Salamonie wasn't in much of a hurry as he readied the canoe and lashed down the gear.

Rain pelted us hard as we finally got under way, and I kept looking at the high tide mark on the distant shoreline. This adventure was not quite over.

The cut finally appeared, and Salamonie finally expressed some emotion.

"Aieeeee," he said. "Maybe not make it. Tide too low."

Vin and I and Madleine looked at each other. It was almost humorous, but we weren't laughing.

"We try anyway," Salamonie said with a big grin. "Maybe get across."

We tried, and we made it, though the prop cleared the rocks by a mere inch or two. Five minutes later and we wouldn't have cleared the cut,

About 10 miles from camp, Salamonie pointed to a small rocky island that couldn't have been more than a quarter mile long. He smiled with a sort of distant look that we didn't understand.

"I born there," he said with pride.

Shaking my head in awe, I couldn't help but be impressed with this rugged lifestyle. These people were survivors, living in some of the harshest environment our planet has to offer.

Closer to the village, Salamonie talked about the Inukshooks that looked down from high ridges. These were rocks piled high, constructed by Eskimos many generations ago to guide travelers along the myriad islands and reefs.

Perhaps the most indelible sight, one which I failed to record with my camera, was a family of Inuits returning from a seal hunt. As they slowly approached the shore with a dead seal draped over the bow, other villagers ran down amidst barking dogs and shouting youngsters. The look of pride on the faces of the victorious hunters was a beautiful sight, each of them beaming and gesturing toward the seal.

Later, when we were standing around in a small group, I noted a young boy looking at me as I whittled on a small caribou rib bone with my pocket knife. He seemed mesmerized by the knife and couldn't take his eyes off it.

Impulsively I closed the blade and offered the knife to the boy. He looked at the knife, then into my eyes, and seemed confused. I gestured with the knife, extending it toward him, but he still couldn't comprehend my intentions. An old man standing next to the boy who might have been his grandfather took the boy's hand and held it toward the knife. I placed it in the boy's hand and saw a look of total joy and happiness in his face. At that he took the knife, shot me a huge grin, and ran off as fast as he could to show it to his pals.

I too had a big smile on my face, and I'll never forget the total sense of satisfaction I had when the boy accepted the knife. It had been a fitting end to a memorable arctic adventure with an incredible race of human beings. I had a tough time getting on the plane. My visit in that wonderful land had been far too short.

HELP, I'M LOST!

Bill Vaznis

Every autumn, three kinds of guys head north to hunt deer in the Adirondacks: Those who never stray more than a few hundred yards from the road: those who venture deep into the forest with map, compass, flashlight and other survival gear: and those who stumble blindly into the darkness without a single clue as to where they are going.

The first two groups of outdoorsmen play it safe and do what it takes to avoid getting "turned around" in the big woods. That other group of nimrods, however, is likely to get lost soon after strolling out of sight. In fact, these "blind stumblers" are often doomed to spending a night in the woods before they ever get started. A few years back, one of those nimrods was me. Let me explain.

I was on a magazine assignment near Old Forge with a couple of friends of mine, including Mark Eddy, a noted Adirondack guide. We began by packing a week's provisions into two canoes early in the day, and then paddling down the Moose River to a campsite known only to Mark, float hunting all the while. It was a good area, he said, full of bucks, and with any luck one of us would tag a real wall-hanger by week's end.

We pitched our tents inside a small cove just before dark, had supper, and then settled down to plan the next day's events under the glare of our gas lanterns.

That's when the ribbing started, and by the tone of the banter, it was going to be a great trip whether we got a buck or not. I especially had a lot of fun teasing Mark about being our guide. Would he stay up all night and keep a fire going for us? How about field dressing our bucks when the time came. Would he do that, too? Mark just growled, waiting for his turn to get even. He knew he had all week.

Then nature called. Well, maybe it was the coffee, but nonetheless, I had to go, so I excused myself and headed out into the darkness to take a dump. I didn't want to spoil the pristine atmosphere of our Adirondack camp, so I decided to get as far away as I dared before I did my duty, thinking all along I could easily find the tent site again by simply looking back for the glow of the lamp light. I should have known better.

Ten minutes later I was ready to head back to the festivities, but I realized I hadn't paid very good atten-

182

tion to where I was going, and in fact didn't have the foggiest notion where the tents were pitched. That's when I noticed it was getting cold, and I didn't bring my jacket. And my flashlight was in my jacket pocket. So was my compass.

Damn! Damn! I said to myself. The camp is only a few hundred yards away, but which direction? Even if I found the river, I could wander up and down its bank all night long. The alders are so thick near the water that I could walk right past the tents and not see them. Then I'd really be in a pickle. I could wait until first light, but that was stupid. Everybody would know I was lost. Besides, I'd probably freeze to death!

There was only one solution, and that was to call for help. But hell, I'd never live it down. I was on top with the ribbing, but only for the present. An event like this could leave me the camp goat for the entire week–something I'd rather avoid. I had to stay calm and think carefully before I did anything.

Then an idea hit me.

"Hey, Mark," I yelled, "Where are you?" No answer, so I yelled a little louder.

"Hey, Mark, where are you?"

Still no answer. Damn, I was really a long way from camp.

"Hey, Mark!" I yelled, this time cupping my hands. "Where are you?"

"What do you want?" he called back.

"Be a good guide and bring me some toilet paper, will you? I left it in my pack."

"Go to hell," he hollered. "If you want it, come back and get it yourself. You'd forget your gun if it didn't have a sling on it."

"Aw, come on," I begged. "Please."

"Drop dead," he answered.

Well, by that time I knew where the campsite was, and eventually strolled back into the light none the worse for the ordeal. I teased Mark a little bit about not meeting all of his customer's needs, and then retired to the warm safety of my sleeping bag, knowing full well my secret was safe. In fact, to this day nobody knows I was lost that night only a few hundred yards from camp.

Mutt Wading

John Barsness

Once upon a time I used to hunt with a tough old Dakota and Assinboine Indian, my first wife's grandfather, who owned a succession of Heinz-57 bird dogs. The first one I knew was a black mutt named Suzie Dump, so named because that's where he found her, on a trip to the local landfill. He swore she was purebred black Lab, but to me she looked remarkably like a cross between a Lab, a coyote, and a greyhound. She acted like none of the above, because her favorite technique was to bounce up and down on top of the wild roses and stunted ash that filled the coulees of northeastern Montana, scaring the wits out of the sharptailed grouse and pheasants under the brush. Our shots were often close, at birds flying right at us, eager to escape the bouncing dumpster.

Suzie begot George, who was stumpier and black-and-white. George liked to chase rocks, so the easiest way to get him to hunt the brush was to toss some rocks into the cover. He was eager for anything, chasing jackrabbits for miles, and if you threw a rock nearby would actually retrieve dead birds, whereas Suzie only mouthed them, then bounced up and down in circles while you waded through the roses to pick up the bird. Evidently, George's few Labrador genes came to the fore, even after Suzie's crossbreeding with a Holstein, or whatever his father was.

One November we decided to jump-shoot some farm ponds for ducks. It was a raw, windy day, with skiffs of dry, piercing snow, and the prairie mallards from Canada had come down. So we loaded up George and headed out. At the second pond, I approached cautiously and managed to drop a drake out of a small flock when they flushed from the other side of the tall cattails.

There was only one problem. Though the water in the middle of the pond was still open, it had frozen a half inch thick amid the cattails, and George couldn't plow his way through, even though I threw rocks out there to inspire him. So I started through in my hip boots, breaking a trail. George couldn't wait. I was ten feet out, feet deep in primordial ooze, when he came after me. I tried to turn and shout him back, but couldn't even twist. He swam right up my jeans pockets, and we both went down in icy black pond water. I was wet to my chest by the time we thrashed back to shore, and I felt like picking up another rock, but didn't. As I

186

stood beside the pickup cab, swearing and dumping the swamp-muck from my hippers, George brought the mallard up and dropped it at my feet. I thought we'd go home so I could change into dry clothes, but my partner had no such thought, and it was his truck. So we rode around, me in my socks with the heater blasting, and eventually I was dry, if somewhat black. I can't remember if we shot any more ducks that day, but George chased some more rocks.

Bruising Battle With a Buck

By Jud McCarty as told to Tom Huggler

Although some of the details are a little fuzzy after 12 years, I remember the date well because my son Jud, Jr., was born a week later. I had used up all my vacation time hunting out West and so had only the mornings to hunt around my home. I believe I hunted opening day. This particular day was my second time in the woods that deer season.

A quarter-mile behind our house is a small lake. The south-side field, which was in corn that year, slopes down to it. On the east side of the lake are some willows and waist-high dead grass – good cover for deer. I took a stand near the end of a north-south fence row. Here I could see the heavy cover, a hundred yards or so away, in front of me and could keep an eye on a deer trail that ran pretty much east and west, between the lake and sloping cornfield.

I was in position by 7 o'clock. It was a crisp morning with a clear sky that promised sun. I knew when the sun came it would be at my back, right where I wanted it. It might sound silly, but I had a feeling that today I'd be lucky. I've had that feeling before, hunting elk out West. It doesn't come very often, maybe once every two or three years. It's strange – I cannot explain it – but it happened on this morning.

I leaned my gun against the fence row, taking care to clear the area of twigs and so forth so I could grab the gun without problem. I remember there was a crabapple tree next to me. As I said, it was cold. My hands were cold, even with brown jersey gloves, and so I stuffed them into my down suit to keep warm.

It was at that moment that I saw the deer. He was coming out of the willows into the tall grass and all I could see were his antlers. They seemed to wave around his head above the tall grass. He was coming straight south, parallel to the fence row where I stood. He was about 100 yards away and coming closer. I had the gun up – I was shooting shotgun slugs – and was just waiting for him to get closer.

When he stepped from the tall grass, he put his head down to sniff the ground. There wasn't much cover here since the corn had been picked. He stopped about 20 yards from the dead grass, maybe 80 yards from me. The deer looked west, presenting a broadside shot, as though he might have heard or seen something. I've hunted deer long enough to know it doesn't take much to spook them. One or two jumps and he could be back in the tall grass and then gone.

I'm used to hunting with a rifle anyway, and in my mind 80 yards was duck soup. So I shot and he went down. He got up, leaped, and I shot again. Down he went again, but by now he was in the dead grass. He jumped up high again, offering a good body shot. I fired a third time and knocked him down a third time. I figured I had hit the deer three times with my 12-gauge slugs. I was using a Remington 870 pump with the Deerslayer barrel.

Apparently I'm not affected by this so-called "buck fever" because I don't remember getting excited – by that or by any other deer – until after I shot. I've never jumped up and yelled or racked shells on the ground, as you hear about. I'm sure it happens, but, fortunately, it has never happened to me.

Anyway, he was down in the grass and I didn't see him jump up anymore. I leaped over the two-wire fence and started running down there. At the same time I was fishing in my pocket for the fourth shell since my gun was now empty. All I had were four shells. Since I had shot three, that meant only one was left. Only I couldn't find it. I figured I had lost it when I cleared the fence, but by now I was almost on top of the deer and didn't want to waste time going back to look for it.

When I got to the buck, he was down but holding
his head up and looking at me. I knew I had hit the
gut. Not only could I see it, but it smelled terrible.
Steam was rising from the wound area. As it turned
out, only my first shot had hit him; the other two had
missed. I knew that with a gut shot a hunter can easily
lose his deer. No bones are hit. No vital organs are hit.
A gut-shot deer doesn't bleed much. I had to find a
way to kill him quickly. I was out of shells and I had
forgotten my knife. I laid down my gun; it was useless
to me.

Nearby I found a rock about 10 inches in diame-
ter. I threw it at his head, but the rock just bounced off.
The deer shook his head and started to get up on his
front feet. His tongue was out and he was panting like
a dog. I had never seen a deer do that before. I figured
maybe I could run a sharp stick down his throat. I
found one and proceeded to do just that, but the deer
shook his head again, swinging those horns around
and catching me on the left forearm. Later I discovered it was bruised.

It was a good warning and I certainly took notice
of those horns. I don't think I was afraid at the time,
but I knew I'd have to be careful. By now the deer had
stopped panting and was up on his front feet and when
I circled around him, he kept his eyes right on me,
glaring. I couldn't think of a way to finish him off. I

192

remember jamming my pockets again, looking for that fourth shell. It wasn't there.

The buck then stood up on all fours and shook his head again. Wobbling, he started to walk away. I thought maybe I could push him over, but he swung those antlers around at me. I stopped and he charged, taking a couple steps toward me. He caught me in his antlers and picked me right up into the air. I grabbed the antlers, but my right hand slipped and he then raked me with his left antler from my right hip to the ribs. Later I had bruises, but luckily he didn't puncture the skin. The attack didn't knock me down, as I remember it, but it sure surprised me!

The deer walked off, unsteadily, and left me standing there, wondering what to do.

By now I was thinking of how we used to dehorn cattle on the farm. We were taught to throw the animal down by twisting its head and wrestling it to the ground where we'd end up on top. When I started chasing the deer, with that thought in mind, he suddenly turned and attacked me again, this time leaping three or four times at me. Again, I grabbed his antlers, slipped off, and he raked me a second time, this time up the front. I remember feeling pain from that attack, but, again, luckily, there was no physical damage. I was on the ground, but he didn't gore me.

I jumped up and remember something catching

my eye. It was the pocket from my torn hunting suit. It was strange seeing it float, almost in slow motion, to the ground.

That attack was certainly more aggressive than the first one. The deer took off again, still heading west along the cornfield slope by the lake. Then he fell down. I ran up to him again, grabbed his antlers and rolled him over on his back. I knew if he got to his feet again I might lose him. My farm experiences had taught me that if you can get a hooved animal on its back, it has no way of getting its feet under it to get up. Watch a film, for example, of a lion or tiger, and you'll see how they knock their prey on their backs so the animals can't get up.

So I held him down. My face was right in his and I remember he had horrible breath. Grunting and groaning, he was breathing deeply and this nauseating odor was in my face. I think it was about then that I decided that I might drown him.

The lake was only 30 or 40 yards away. I stopped a couple of times, while dragging him there, when he began kicking, but I don't remember him pulling that hard. There was a skim of ice on the lake. I dragged him out about 10 feet into a foot of water and lay right on top of him. He was still on his back but his nose was sticking up. When the cold water hit him, he really started struggling and kicking. I waited a moment for him to stop and then dragged him out another few feet to maybe two feet of water.

Now I was lying in water right up to my neck. His strugglings seemed to subside; so I relaxed a bit. Suddenly he curled his body like a tomato worm and those two hind feet came out of the water and started zinging over my head. Right at that point, for the first time, I wondered what I was doing out there. I was getting worried. The shock of being in ice water and the fact that I was exhausted began to affect me. I couldn't do any more and was about to give up. But about that time his strugglings began to get weaker. That encouraged me; so I just lay there with my head low. In another minute or so the air bubbles stopped. I stood up, fell down, and stood up again. The deer didn't move. Grabbing his antlers, I dragged him to shore, where I just sat with my feet still in the water.

Suddenly he started to gasp. In hindsight, I suppose it was just a vacuum of air or whatever in his lungs, but it startled me. I jumped up and dragged him back into the water where I then lay on him again for another minute or two.

It probably sounds kind of nuts, but I had gone this far and now I would do whatever I had to to tag that buck. I dragged him back to shore. It was then that I remembered to make sure his tongue was hanging out, the certain sign of a dead animal. It may have been out before I dragged him back into the lake, but I just didn't think to check.

As I said, I had no knife to dress him out. On the walk home, I looked for that fourth shell but never did find it. Back home, I shocked my pregnant wife BJ. She saw that I was wet and had blood all over me and that my hunting suit was torn. She said my eyes were as big as saucers. I briefly told her what happened and changed my clothes. Then I grabbed my hunting knife and drove the tractor back to the lake and the deer. Upon dressing him out, I noticed his lungs were heavy and full of water.

I was now at least dry, but I was really beat and had trouble loading him onto the back of the tractor. It was all coming into perspective by now and I realized that what had happened was unreal. I was lucky I hadn't been hurt really bad.

On the ride back to the barn, I got chilled. So I took a hot shower, drank two cups of coffee, and rested for about a half-hour. Then I drove to Lakeville High School where my father was teaching. I got him out into the hallway and told him the story.

I remember two things he said. The first was, "I'll be damned." The second was also, "I'll be damned."

Later I took the buck to Smith's Meats, a local slaughterhouse, to be butchered. R. J. Smith and Joe Barden skinned the deer and cut off its head and legs.

Then they decided to weigh it. The carcass weighed 222 pounds. A chart I have at the bank where I work is supposedly pretty accurate for estimating animal weights. Taking into consideration the hide, head, and legs. he would have weighed live between 325 and 350 pounds. R.J., who has butchered animals all his life, agrees with that estimate.

As I look back on my experience, I don't think it was a wise or safe thing to do. Under the same circumstances I wouldn't do it again. Then again I wouldn't let it happen again. I try to be better prepared now by carrying extra shells, in my inside blue jeans pocket and not in the outside pockets where they can be lost. And I won't leave the yard when hunting without carrying my knife.

A wounded deer is a very dangerous animal.

The Colonel's Best from Chicken, Alaska

Craig Boddington

Back in 1975 I was an enterprising, though fairly unsuccessful, freelance writer. I was *also* a totally addicted hunter, far beyond hope. I was also a Second Lieutenant in our United States' own Marine Corps. Now, I loved the Corps then as a second looie or butter bar (only in the Army do they call them "El Tee"). I love it still as an increasingly senior Lieutenant Colonel, albeit Reserve. But I doubt if I ever loved it more when, in July of that year, my Company Commander informed me that I had to pack my gear and go to Alaska for two months.

Now, I knew that my Company Commander – a god-like, omnipotent, and ancient figure – merely wanted to get rid of me. Read "god like" in the Old Testament sense: his "welcome aboard" to newly reporting Lieutenant Boddington was to tell me that, since I did not have prior enlisted service – and he did – I was worthless, less than useless, and I would be

disposed of at the earliest opportunity. And, having
received his welcome, I must get out of his sight. Read
"omnipotent" any way you choose, or, better, go watch
"A Few Good Men" one more time. Things were different in those post-Vietnam days. My Company
Commander's policy was that, if a troop needed
"thumping" *he* would do it himself. Read "ancient"
from the standpoint of a still-21-year-old Second
Lieutenant. My god-like, omnipotent, ancient
Company Commander was still well shy of 30. But as
the only, unfortunately, non-prior enlisted Platoon
Commander in his company – and, fortunately, as the
only *single* Platoon Commander in his company – I'd
spent six months of seven-day weeks and 20-hour days
creating, with the help of some really super sergeants,
the best rifle platoon in the world. At least to us. And
at least he hadn't found the excuse he needed to get
rid of me. But a school quota was a school quota, so
the next best thing was to banish me to the frozen
North for August and September. To this day he probably wonders why I didn't try to worm out of it.

Just tonight, when delving into a desk drawer full
of old papers, I found the handwritten manuscript that
resulted from that trip – officially, to attend the Army's
Arctic Military Mountaineering (Summer) Course at
Fort Greeley, south of Fairbanks near Delta Junction.
The story, perhaps the most forgettable I've ever

written, was published in *Fur-Fish-Game* under the title "Where The Heck Is Chicken, Alaska." (I'm reasonably sure I typed it before submitting.) I never saw a printed version, since I was posted overseas when it appeared. I also hadn't read the manuscript for nearly 20 years, and the only thing familiar was the horrible handwriting.

Well, it's best to forget the manuscript, whatever it looked like in print. I had two months of prime time in Alaska, courtesy of Uncle Sam. A few fish got caught, maybe enough to make an almost-story—but nothing four-footed came close to being in danger. And, for our purposes, *that* is the story.

I had visions of Dall sheep dancing before my eyes. While I was packing I took time to jot down some phone numbers from "Where To Go" sections of hunting magazines. I knew I'd only have a few weekends free, but in the spirit of optimism I figured I might find an out-of-work guide who would give me a military discount for a short hunt. In the same spirit the first thing I did in Alaska was to trot down to the Fort Greeley PX and plunk down cash for a nonresident hunting license and sheep tag. Of course, they shouldn't have sold it to me without a registered guide's name affixed – but they didn't know that, and neither did I.

Equally of course, every guide within 200 miles

was either out in the bush or out of my very low price range. But that proved to be nothing unusual in those days of Alaska's pipeline boom – *everything* was out of my price range.

Oh, I went sheep hunting. Sort of. One of the instructors, a legal resident, was after a ram and we backpacked into the nearby mountains on the August weekends hoping to fill his tag. Mine was out of the question. The senior instructor, a Major, had already taken me aside and told me – in no uncertain terms – that I was not to even think about filling that sheep tag unless I could find a licensed guide to accompany me. We never saw any rams on those weekend jaunts. But I did see plenty of sheep. We saw them every weekday while we learned glacier crossings, river crossings, rock climbing, technical rope work, and all kinds of things that took up precious hunting time.

Finally August passed into September, bringing in moose and caribou season. After a month of five-dollar hamburgers and three dollar beers I was out of any potential guide money, let alone tag money – but in that wonderful and peculiar quirk of Alaskan law my totally useless sheep license was now good for any tag of equal or lesser value. Back in business.

With a borrowed .303 Enfield, I combed the low marshes for an unsuspecting moose. None of these moose were unsuspecting. There were plenty of tracks – old. And plenty of droppings – also old. But the only moose seen were, again, during the weekdays when, having finished with glaciers and such, we were learning boat work on the Tanana River.

Then came a three-day weekend. One of the instructors, Staff Sergeant Jim Tynes, heard that caribou were crossing the highway not far from Chicken, Alaska. (Halfway from Tok to Eagle, of course.) Why not?

At the last minute Tynes was called out on a mountain search and-rescue mission, but he offered his old Dodge truck and his new .270. I had enough sense to find an accomplice, Marine Sergeant John Mattingly. He didn't have enough sense to decline. So, with maps in hand, we headed southeast to Tok and on north to Chicken.

We stopped at a lonely gas station to fill up, and I dug in the surrounding junk searching in vain for a spare tire that would fit the Dodge. That effort failed, and so did our attempt to get any information about these passing herds of caribou. "Caribou? Sure, over that way."

"How far?"

"About a thousand miles over toward Northwest Territories." We passed through Chicken proper – three houses, a school, and a post officer – and continued up the winding gravel highway, visions of bald tires and

no spare dancing through my mind. A long ways
north, along the Hell's Roaring River, we came to a
gas station cum cafe cum bar. We did the natural thing
and went into the bar, receiving the same news about
the still-distant caribou herds. Then a wiry, bearded
fellow in the uniform flannel shirt and Levi's took pity
on us. He had a gold mining claim upriver a little
ways, and he told us that the real migration was indeed
a month away. But he also told us of a small resident
herd not too far away – just perhaps reachable from
the highway, depending on where they were.

It was too late to make a start that afternoon, so
our new friend – Buck Jones by name – led us to his
cabin. Grayling were running well right then, and with
fly rods unlimbered we caught supper in just a few
minutes. In the morning we caught a few more fish
and panned a few flakes of yellow gold from the Hell's
Roaring. We should have been long gone and covering
ground if we hoped to find caribou, but I think we
already knew it was futile.

Eventually, though, we dug out our maps and got
directions, then drove a few miles north to Buck's suggested starting point. The day had dawned overcast,
and by now, midmorning, dense fog lay over the
tundra. We left the truck and climbed the first ridge.
Only blind luck – or perhaps the nagging thought that
I'd done something terribly wrong – made me turn

around before we topped the first ridge. The pale glow from the Dodge's headlights cut dimly through the fog. I climbed back down and cut the lights, and finally we topped the ridge and headed southwest by compass.

At that time I had hunted several times in British Columbia, but never before on foot in tundra. This was real tundra, but not flat tundra. Ridges rose and fell away into deep valleys one after another – it was the most hellish walking I can remember, even though I was almost certainly in the best shape of my life. The fog made it worse, for we were walking in a gray world that gave no glimpse of what lay ahead.

Perhaps there were caribou around, but no way would we ever know. Certainly there were tracks, and droppings that seemed fairly fresh. But the fog limited us to a few yards – and we were altogether too stubborn to admit we were wasting our breath, literally, as well as our time. We walked in our gray world for six hours, and we might have passed every caribou in the state of Alaska. Or none at all. Somehow, around four in the afternoon, our course began to describe a big circle. Then, without any conscious decision being made and with no thought of the sleeping bags and C-Rations we carried, we followed our back azimuth toward the highway.

We stumbled onto it about ten in the evening, in a gray twilight made grayer by the persistent fog. The

Dodge was there. It started right up and carried us straight to Buck Jones' bunkhouse — where we should have stayed in the first place. Next morning's reveille was a .30-06 fired over the bunkhouse — but the first shot failed to rouse us, the second drew only grumbles, and only the third brought us out of our comas.

We caught some more grayling and panned a bit more gold that morning, then started the long drive back to Fort Greeley. We arrived none too soon, for the Army had already sounded the alarm over two missing Marines. I was the senior, so I took the blame and the dressing down. It didn't bother me much. These guys tried to look stern, but weren't in the same league with the Company Commander I'd have to face on my return.

A couple of weekends of fruitless moose hunting remained, and then we did indeed have to head back to the Lower 48, my unfilled sheep tag my best souvenir. I at least knew where Chicken, Alaska was. I knew, too — and 20 years later I still know — that unguided Alaskan hunting requires lots of time, lots of patience, and a total disregard for success!

There's No Such Thing as a Free Dog!

Roy Schara

The first hunting dog I ever a owned cost me $20. That's not a large amount of money unless you're 12 years old, which I was. My first dog meant going into debt.

Little did I know, decades later, I'd still be making doggie payments. No matter what the newspaper ads say, free (or cheap) puppies and dogs are like free lunches. There's no such thing.

My own venture into debt began with Taffy, a light-blonde Cocker Spaniel with a great nose for birds, cockleburs and fresh cow pies.

Despite her cow-pasture wandering, Taffy could do no wrong in my young eyes. She was always full of surprises. Sometimes she'd even come when called. She was really a birdy dog, too. If she smelled the scent of a pheasant, hot or cold, she'd follow that bird to the next county—and often did. I would have had lots of pheasants if I could have run a little faster.

Thanks to Taffy, I saw lots of birds out of range. Probably just as well. If the pheasant had been close, I'd have probably missed anyway. To paraphrase W.C. Fields, there's never a hunting dog so bad that it can't serve as a good example.

Thinking of Taffy reminds me of a black Lab named Fancy.

Fancy belonged to Bob, a friend of mine, who eventually realized that as a hunting dog, Fancy was anything but.

You could say Fancy was unique, a retriever who hated to retrieve. All of which explains why one morning, as we were about to go duck hunting, Bob decided to leave Fancy in the motel room.

I was particularly overjoyed by the decision. And I knew Bob was relieved, too. It was the best and easiest choice. Fancy loved to sleep in Bob's bed. Being a laid-back dog, we also knew Fancy wouldn't bother the maid when she came to clean the room .

As it turned out, the maid didn't even try to make the bed or open the curtains. For one thing, she couldn't find the drapes. Well, not right away.

Fancy must have torn down the curtains shortly after we left so she'd see Bob leave. We can only guess why she wanted to dig through the mattress. Probably thought she could dig her way out and find Bob. She was as far as the bedsprings when the maid knocked.

When we returned from duck hunting, we should have known something was wrong. It was still early, yet everybody was up, including the motel manager, who was waiting to greet us. We thought he wanted to see our ducks. But when he started talking to Bob, his teeth and lips barely moved. His nose was gasping like a pressure cooker gauge.

Obviously, the task of managing a motel had shattered his nerves. When he pointed at Fancy, his hands shook, poor fella.

To Bob's credit, he apologized for everything Fancy did, including the fit of barking just before sunrise.

Bob didn't argue over the $300 bill, either. Oh, he could have protested the drape charges, I suppose. Actually, Fancy had only shredded one pair of drapes, leaving the other curtain somewhat messy but easily cleaned.

Certainly, the manager wasn't exaggerating over the condition of the mattress. On that, Bob agreed, too. Its twin size had been halved by a gaping hole.

The door also was damaged, although Bob said it's amazing how teeth and claw marks will disappear with a little sandpaper and wood filler.
No dogs are perfect, of course.

For example, I'll never forget the day the Brittany Spaniel puppy I had ordered showed up at the house.

I'd bought the pup sight unseen from a professional dog trainer.

It was the cutest little black puppy.

Yes, I know Brittany Spaniels are not supposed to have black coats. While my daughters kissed and hugged the pup, I frantically called the trainer. He said the pup was "a little dark" but should lighten up as it got older. If not, he said, I could bring the pup back and get a Brittany that looked like a Brittany.

A day later it was too late to think of exchanging pups. My daughters had developed an iron-like attachment to the pup, naming the dog Kelly.

Three dog trainers tried in vain to make Kelly act like a Brittany. But she didn't care about birds.

Garbage? Well that's another story . . .

Warden's Dog

Chuck Petrie

As I led the handcuffed prisoner up the brushy stream bank toward my squad car, our exhalations appeared as clouds of condensation in the cold night air. He was a tall man with a massive upper body and muscular arms—and a disproportionately small head. With his full black beard he reminded me of Brutus in the old "Popeye" comic strip. He wasn't happy about having to go to jail, and although he maintained his composure thus far, I had the gut feeling he could be one of those volatile prisoners who, once inside the squad car, would begin to thrash, kick and curse all the way to the sheriff's office. Sometimes, transporting a prisoner can be more difficult than making the actual arrest, and this guy already seemed put out that I hadn't allowed him to spear walleyes all night. As we walked, I thought I could hear him gnashing his teeth.

I opened the front passenger's door to put the man in the squad car. There, in the passenger seat, lay Keyni (pronounced "keen-eye"), my black Lab. I signalled the dog with a hand motion and commanded, "Back seat, Keyni." The dog climbed into the center of the back seat and quietly sat down, facing the front of the car. I put the Brutus in the passenger's seat, connected his seatbelt and closed the door.

As I climbed into the driver's seat, I noticed the man's demeanor had changed. He sat twisted part way around and apprehensively eyed Keyni. The dog, in turn, was staring that intense, inscrutible brown-eyed Labrador retriever stare directly into Brutus' face. "Uh . . . hey, warden, does that dog bite?"

I started the engine, dropped the shift lever into drive and steered the big Dodge onto the road. Looking over at the man, I answered in as nonchalant a tone as I could, "Only on command."

Of course, the only thing the walleye thief had to fear was that Keyni might jump in his lap and lick him into a coma. But that was for him to find out. It was a quiet ride to the jail.

During my ten years as a game warden, I was constantly amazed at how effective Keyni was as a patrol partner. Either through sheer intimidation, (most law-breakers seemed to assume Keyni was trained for K-9 duties as an attack dog, evidence "sniffer" and tracker, etc.) or by retrieving illegal game, he earned his stripes as a deputy. Actually, he received no special training, only that which most men give their dogs for hunting purposes. Keyni just seemed to have a knack for warden duty.

Over the years, Keyni accompanied me on expeditions for ducks, geese, grouse, and pheasants. He was an all-around hunter-retriever and less bullheaded and obstinate than the average dog of his breed, although, as will be revealed, he did have his moments.

The dog was also my constant companion. He lived in my house; he slept at the foot of my bed; he rode with me in squad cars and patrol boats, and he even staked out his own private corner in my office at the area DNR headquarters. This constant association sometimes made me wonder if I wasn't subliminally emulating one of my boyhood heroes, Sergeant Preston of the Northwest Mounted Police. The indomitable mountie always had his canine sidekick, Yukon King, fighting crime by his side in the wilds of Canada. Many an illegal trapper, poacher, murderer or thief was brought to justice with the aid of the faithful malamute, and I still remember Sergeant Preston signing off the old radio program with: "Well, King, another case closed."

Actually, all I originally wanted was just a good bird dog. After receiving my permanent commission as a Wisconsin Conservation Warden, I was assigned to Horicon on the southern end of Wisconsin's famous Horicon Marsh. I was single, living in a rented farmhouse on the edge of the marsh and was surrounded by prime pheasant and waterfowl habitat. To take advantage of the bird hunting opportunities, I decided to acquire a Lab. Shortly after getting settled in my new station, I put out the word that I was looking for a dog. Within a few weeks I had one. The parents of a young man who was going off to college just didn't have time for their son's dog. They were looking for a good home for a one-year-old black Lab male named Keyni.

One of Keyni's first "cases" came that spring when I received a telephone call regarding Mischievous Melvin, one of our local trappers. The caller related that Melvin was down at his boathouse on one of the marsh channels, plinking at coots with a pellet gun. Melvin, the caller said, would usually let the dead coots lay until nightfall, then paddle his skiff out and retrieve them.

Melvin was a wily and cantankerous old marshrat. He had earned his nickname from years of walking a fine edge between a life of poaching and law-and-order. When Melvin wasn't holding down a steady job, which was most of the time, he was on the marsh hunting, fishing or trapping—and sometimes all three at once. He wasn't a dangerous fellow, just shifty, and I knew he could probably cook a coot to taste like a filet mignon.

As soon as I got off the telephone, Keyni and I drove off, hoping to catch Mischievous in in the act. Ten minutes later, I had parked my squad at a boat landing about a block from Melvin's boathouse and was sneaking along a row of trappers' shanties and small boathouses toward Melvin's wood-frame shack. Keyni stalked quietly at heel. When we arrived at the door of the shack, I could hear movement inside.

The door to the boathouse was slightly ajar. I peeked inside. There, surrounded by shelves of decoys, traps, push-poles, marsh skis and various piles of hunting, fishing and trapping paraphernalia, sat Melvin, laboriously pumping the handle of a pellet rifle. He was getting ready to snipe his next victim.

I looked through the boathouse and beyond the open swing-out door on the opposite side of the shack. From inside, Melvin could sit unobserved and pot any unsuspecting coot that paddled by. Across the water-filled channel behind the boat house was a large cattail stand. A couple of mudhens were milling around in the green shoots of the young vegetation.

Mischievous was just about to take a bead on one of the coots when the wind suddenly blew the door open, revealing Keyni and me in the doorway. Melvin heard the noise and jerked his head around in our direction.

"AND WHAT THE HELL DO YOU WANT?"

he demanded loudly.

Having lost the element of surprise and feeling somewhat chagrined at being caught eavesdropping, I stepped into the boathouse and confronted him. "Caught you shooting coot out of season . . . eh, Melvin?"

"There ain't no law against shootin' a pellet gun in the water, warden. Is there?"

He had me there. As I looked across the water, I couldn't see any dead coot, and I hadn't gotten the chance to see him shoot at a live one.

"We'll see, Melvin, we'll see," I bluffed.

I looked down at Keyni. He was staring out the door at the vegetation across the channel.

"Keyni, DEAD BIRD!" I commanded, and out the open door he went, plunging into the water. He headed straight for the cattails.

I had no idea if there were any dead coot out there, and I had no idea if the dog would make a blind retrieve. But Keyni seemed to know what was expected of him; he immediately began swimming around in the cattails when he reached the other side of the channel. I looked at Mischievous Melvin. As he glowered at Keyni quartering about in the vegetation, Mischievous began to look a little sick, and his pallor began to change like a kid who had eaten too much candy.

In less than a minute of searching, Keyni was swimming back to the boathouse with a dead coot in his jaws. He crawled up the old board that served as a boat ramp and dropped the bird in my hand.

"A dead coot don't prove nothin'!" Melvin spit the words out along with a stream of Plowboy that landed with a "SPLAT" on the floor of the wooden shed.

"Maybe not, Melvin, maybe not."

I pulled out my pocket knife and began probing the blade in what appeared to be a wound channel in the bird's neck. It didn't take long to make a retrieve of my own, a .177 cal. pellet. I held the incriminating bloody missile between my thumb and forefinger and, smiling, displayed it to Melvin. He sat down, letting the pellet gun fall to the floor.

Mischievous was crestfallen. "Oh, what the hell," he lamented, "you might as well send that dam dog out to pick up the other two." I did.

Of course, Keyni's virtues were balanced at times with the character flaws peculiar to all black Labs: There were times when he seemed deaf, defiant and incorrigible. One of these periods occurred one fall day when we were creeping up on some hunters who were pass shooting at ducks and geese from the edge of a woodlot near the marsh. As we stole closer to them, I could make out the hunters, two boys in their mid-teens and a younger boy of about twelve. The kids had a huge, mean looking Chesapeake Bay retriever with them.

After watching the boys shoot at some astounding ranges for a few more minutes, I decided to check their licenses and give them some pointers on shotgun ballistics and range estimation. Considering Keyni's pugilistic tendencies and the presence of the Chesapeake, however, I decided to leave him at our surveillance point. I told him "stay" and started walking toward the young hunters.

I hadn't gone thirty feet before Keyni was slinking along by my side. "Stay!" I whispered to him as loudly and sternly as I could and started off again. I was about ninety feet from the hunters when I noticed Keyni trailing quietly behind me once more. I grabbed him by the collar, shook him and told him again, "Stay, you bum!"

The kids didn't even know I was there until I stepped out of the woods behind them. I identified myself as a warden and asked to see their licenses. There were properly licensed, and their shotguns were plugged for hunting waterfowl, but I found they had been shooting trap loads at ducks and geese at a range I estimated to be over 70 yards. The boys had been pretty quiet up to this point. It was probably the first time they had been checked by a warden, and I assumed they were a little nervous.

I had decided to give them the "officer friendly" approach and a talk on shotshell capabilities when Keyni suddenly appeared from the brush and sat down in front of me. The dog had disobeyed again. I was furious. Without a word, I leaned over and grabbed him by the loose skin above his shoulders with one hand and by the skin of his rump with the other. I intended to pick him up off his feet and shake him soundly while scolding him.

But I was a little overzealous and a little off balance when I picked him up, and as I lifted him I had to take two quick steps backward to keep my feet. My second step ended abruptly against a fallen tree limb, though, and before I knew it I was falling backward. Keyni, still firmly in my grasp, passed before my eyes, going up and over my head as I went into a fully extended rear prat-fall, looking not unlike a football referee signalling a touchdown while hold-ing a writhing black Labrador — at least for that frac-tion of a second before we both crashed to the ground.

I got up, embarrassed and thirsty for blood: Labrador retriever blood. The muscles in my cheeks bulged and I could feel my fingernails dig into my palms as I rolled my fists. I had the wide-eyed stare of a man about to commit mayhem. Then I remembered the boys were there.

"Sir, can we go now?" the oldest one asked apprehensively. They all appeared shocked, even the Chesapeake's jaw was hanging open, a look of frightened bewilderment was in its eyes.

"Yeah . . . sure, kids, go ahead." I didn't feel like "officer friendly" anymore, so I decided to save it for another day. The kids seemed almost to run as they disappeared into the woods toward town.

That night I received a telephone call from a concerned parent. The caller told me that his two sons and one of their friends had been hunting and were approached by a man impersonating a warden.

"What happened?" I asked.

"Well, the boys said this guy dressed in a uniform checked their licenses and guns. They really thought he was a game warden. Then, they said, a dog walked out of nowhere and this man went berserk. He picked the dog up and threw it into the air over his head and told the boys, 'Get out of here.' The kids were pretty scared. They ran all the way home. Warden, the boys think this guy stayed out there and killed that dog."
As the man spoke, Keyni was snoozing on my living room rug, digesting a belly full of warm dog food and leftover steak and occasionally emitting a satisfying belch.

"Can the boys identify this man?" I inquired uneasily.

"All they can remember is that he was big, mean-looking, and that his face got real red when he saw that dog."

"That's not much to go on, sir, but I'll investigate the matter and get back to you if I find out anything. Thanks for calling."

Keyni was instrumental in helping me arrest a number of other violators during the years I was stationed at Horicon. Of course, bureaucracies being what they are—and the DNR being no exception—Keyni never got any official recognition for his efforts. At least none that the bureaucrats are aware of.

There is an old warden proverb that says: "When your arrest reports arrive at the state capitol, the brass don't read 'em, they just file 'em." I don't know if that's true or not, but now that Keyni is gone, but certainly not forgotten, and I have long since retired from state service, I'll tell you . . . if anybody ever goes through those old arrest reports very carefully, they'll find a certain Labrador retriever listed as "assisting officer" on more than a dozen of them, and somewhere in the long narrative portion of at least one of those reports they'll find the words: "Well, Keyni, another case closed."

221